THE INVESTOR'S GOLDEN PLAYBOOK

12 RULES FOR ACHIEVING REAL WEALTH

written by 40 YEAR VETERAN FINANCIAL ADVISOR

FRANK J. BUCHHOLZ

The inside secrets to successful investing and money management, including 401(k)s. It's *not* complicated!

investorsgoldenplaybook.com

ISBN: 979-8-9920640-0-1 (paperback)
ISBN: 979-8-9920640-1-8 (ebook)
ISBN: 979-8-9920640-2-5 (hardcover)

Printed in: Huntington Beach, CA

Library of Congress Control Number: 2024925204

Ordering Information:
Special discounts are available on quantity purchases by corporations, associations, and others. For details, contact investorsgoldenplaybook.com

Publisher's Cataloging-in-Publication Data:

Names: Buchholz, Frank J., 1952- .
Title: The investor's golden playbook : 12 rules for achieving real wealth / Frank J. Buchholz.
Description: Huntington Beach, CA : Frank Buchholz, 2025. | Summary: Inside secrets for successful retirement planning, investing, and money management, including 401(k)s.
Identifiers: LCCN 2024925204 | ISBN 9798992064025 (hardcover) | ISBN 9798992064018 (ebook)
Subjects: LCSH: Finance, Personal – United States. | Investments. | Saving and investment. | Retirement – planning. | BISAC: BUSINESS & ECONOMICS / Personal Finance / Money Management. | BUSINESS & ECONOMICS / Personal Finance / Investing. | BUSINESS & ECONOMICS / Personal Finance / Retirement Planning.
Classification: LCC HG179.B83 2025 | DDC 332.024 B--dc23
LC record available at https://lccn.loc.gov/2024925204

This book is dedicated to my four favorite ladies. My loving and beautiful wife, Beverly, my two incredibly special daughters, Jessica and Melissa, and our precious little corgi, Miss Maggie.

CONTENTS

INTRODUCTION

The More You Learn the More You Earn

This book is all about helping you to achieve your vision of financial success—now and into the future. The chapters ahead present the golden rules that will help you realize and enjoy that success throughout the course of your life. My goal is to provide the information you need to live well, retire comfortably, and enjoy a life that is free of money worries. As a retired wealth manager, I'm happy and grateful to say that I have achieved that goal, and I know you can too if you follow the 12 golden rules of money and investing you'll find in this book.

To illustrate my methodology, I've included stories from my own career. Over the years, I've dealt with some remarkably successful folks who followed the rules and made their money work for them. I'll tell you about them, but I've also included stories about people who made some pretty disastrous decisions and consequently lost a fortune. They thought the golden rules of money didn't apply to them. They were wrong. The rules of money apply equally to everyone.

This is my simple investment philosophy, just 12 tried-and-true rules—developed over a lifetime—that have reliably produced more than 10% annual returns for my clients, year in and year out. With a long enough time horizon, that rate of return will grow into a sizable cushion that will allow you to live in comfort, free from money woes, even once it's time to quit working and enjoy your golden years.

I started my 401(k) in 1986 and ended it in 2021. Over the course of that time, incrementally, I invested approximately $770,000 of my hard-earned dollars. Today my retirement account is worth over $8.5 million! I will show you exactly what I did to achieve this impressive result. And while your retirement might seem like it's a long way off—and those numbers might seem impossibly large to you now—I'm here to tell you, life is short and money grows, *if you let it!*

It's not that complicated when you get right down to dollars and common sense. Consider this—would you rather have two cups of Starbucks coffee every day or $1 million in the bank? I think we both know the answer to that question. In this book, I'll show you an easy way to achieve that goal of $1 million just by putting aside your coffee allowance—small change—for two cups of Starbucks each and every day. Like I said, this is not rocket science. Your contributions can be relatively small, but over time the results are huge if you follow a few simple philosophical rules.

Remember, there are only four ways to become affluent:

1. Inherit your loot.
2. Win the lottery.
3. Rob a bank.
4. Invest your hard-earned money wisely.

Obviously, if you're not a thief, a scion, or particularly lucky, the best way to build wealth is to invest. That is what I did, and now I'm going to show you how I grew my small change into a considerable cushion. I consider these rules and this book to be my legacy. I would like to do my small part to help create a new generation of financially secure Americans who know how to save, invest their money prudently, reap the rewards of their efforts, and give a little something back to the world.

I started my career in the financial services industry in the early 1980s, the era of excess when *Dynasty* was one of the most popular shows on TV, Wall Street was booming, and greed was good. During that raucous time in financial services, I worked for a moderate but well-respected firm called Smith Barney—the home of khakis, blue Oxford-cloth button-down collar shirts, and measured thoughtful investments. You may remember our spokesperson, John Houseman, the professorial and venerable face of the brand, who articulated our motto, “We make money the old-fashioned way, we *earn* it!” And we did. I certainly did.

I passed the Series 7 exam, an arduous and painful deal every investment professional must endure, just as lawyers must pass the bar. I got the notice that I’d passed just before Thanksgiving in 1982, and boy was I thankful that year. The very next day, I was already cold calling people, offering them municipal bonds paying more than 10%. Those were the Wild West days of finance when there were few regulations, and you could cold call anyone to sell them anything without repercussions of any kind from Uncle Sam. Financial management was more about sales than good sound advice. It was a perilous time, which was why an old-fashioned, reliable brand like Smith Barney was appealing to investors.

I stayed at Smith Barney until January 1985. Candidly, I was probably not the best cold caller in the business and, having made 100+ cold calls a day during the previous two+ years, I don’t mind telling you I was *way* over it! There had to be a better way to succeed in the investment arena. If there wasn’t, well then, I needed to find another line of work. I found my better path when I went to work for Security Pacific National Bank in downtown Los Angeles. They were acquired by Bank of America in 1991[1] and then Bank of America acquired Merrill Lynch in the fall of 2008.[2] I remember vividly the day that happened—I was watching the Denver Broncos on TV and my wife yelled out, "You won't believe what just happened!" I still don't remember who won that game.

I guess you could say that after being in the financial industry for nearly 40 years, with all manner of private clients, I really have seen it all, from mergers to meltdowns, soaring booms to spectacular busts. I was there in 1987 when the market crashed 22.6% in one day![3] I was there for the tech wreck around the year 2000 and the Great Recession in 2008 and 2009. I've seen money come, I've seen it go, and I've watched the way people—some wise, some not so savvy—make decisions in light of both windfalls and catastrophes. And I'm not excluding myself from this roundup of American financial low-lights. I watched the shares of Bank of America, *the company I worked for*, go from a closing price of $38.14 a share on October 5, 2007 to a closing price of $2.50 a share on March 6, 2009 in a virtual blink of an eye during the Great Recession.[4]

The industry has changed dramatically over the course of the last four decades. When I started it was basically a sales-driven business offering investment products. Now it's more about offering advice, really getting to know your client, and coming back to him or her with a sound proposal for how you would manage their estate

---

1 Tom Furlong, "Security Pacific: A History," *Los Angeles Times*, April 22, 1992, https://www.latimes.com/archives/la-xpm-1992-04-22-fi-632-story.html.

2 Pratik Patel, "Bank of America's Takeover of Merrill Lynch," Seven Pillars Institute, accessed September 27, 2024, https://sevenpillarsinstitute.org/case-studies/bank-of-americas-takeover-of-merrill-lynch/.

3 Donald Bernhardt and Marshall Eckblad, "Stock Market Crash of 1987," Federal Reserve History, November 22, 2013, https://www.federalreservehistory.org/essays/stock-market-crash-of-1987.

4 "Price History," Bank of America, accessed September 27, 2024, https://investor.bankofamerica.com/shareholder-information/historical-data.

planning, establish a trust, fund their children's college education, choose life insurance, and so much more. This is good news for the client. The investor today is much better served and given significantly better advice and far greater value than when I started.

A fellow financial advisor at the start of my career told me, "You will learn from your clients. They will teach you everything you need to know." Nothing has turned out to be truer. Through the years I have learned so much from my clients—what to do, what not to do, how to gracefully enjoy success, and how to bounce back when you face headwinds. And now I'm going to share stories about these remarkable folks with you.

Alongside these stories you will discover a step-by-step guide to achieving financial well-being at every stage of your life. Honestly, it isn't that complicated. Sound financial practice and following the tried-and-true, golden rules that never go out of style are still the best approaches to solvency. These are the rules your grandfather or grandmother might have told you, just like my grandparents told me. Rules like earning more than you spend and setting something aside for a rainy day might sound outdated and trite, but they are also timeless and true.

I will leave you with two wise thoughts. One is attributed to one of my favorite founding fathers, Benjamin Franklin, who knew a lot about wealth creation: "An investment in knowledge pays the best interest." I wholeheartedly concur. Information is power, and power is treasure. My favorite saying: "The best investment you can make is an investment in yourself. The more you learn, the more you earn."

The only way to achieve real wealth is to spend less than you earn and invest the difference wisely. So, let's get started.

GOLDEN RULE 1

DEVELOP A PROSPERITY MINDSET

Balance Your Life, Balance Your Budget

The most influential and memorable client of my career was a gentleman by the name of Leo Arena, a guy who quite simply did everything right. I had the pleasure of meeting Leo while I was working in private banking at Bank of America in Palm Springs. We met for the first time in June of 1995 and hit it off immediately. A retired dentist, Leo was a robust and vibrant spirit, and I could tell after speaking with him for just a few minutes that he was also a very savvy and successful investor.

Acutely intelligent, Leo was completely passionate about investing in the stock market. He loved it. It had been his main hobby in life since he retired, and that is exactly how he treated it. In the same way that some of my other retired professionals would travel or take up photography or golf, Leo's hobby was conquering the stock market, and he did it with joy in his heart and a skip in his step. I wanted to know how he could invest in a volatile market in the second half of his life and still maintain his serenity and unflappable joie de vivre. I resolved to find out. And so, I started to watch how Leo Arena administered his funds.

The first thing I discovered was that Leo was not just any retired dentist. He was an incredibly wise and shrewd investor. This was part of his secret—he was investing money he could afford to put at risk. He did not have to worry because he never had to sell himself short. Leo had spent prudently, saved diligently, and now had plenty of backup funds. His other secret was that he rarely if ever sold what he bought—he was strictly a buy-and-hold investor.

Although retired, Leo seemed to be in his prime. I thought he was in his seventies—albeit remarkably preserved—when we first met and only later discovered he was already in his early nineties. Leo was always well dressed, had a profound sense of humor, and was deservedly confident about his investment decisions. He saw the upside of everything and was always on the hunt for a bargain. One time while I was visiting Leo it began to rain and he said, "Well, now I'll get a free car wash." The man who had the largest investment account with me was still counting his nickels. This should tell you something. Every nickel matters.

Leo and I became good friends over the years, and I learned a tremendous amount from him about life and about the stock market. I hope he learned as much about bonds from me, although I don't think my game was as interesting to him as his was to me. I can still remember him telling me he didn't understand bonds. I thought to myself, what's to understand? Bonds are easy. You have a maturity date, you get paid twice a year, and you get your money back when the bonds mature. I finally realized that what he couldn't understand was why anybody would buy bonds because there is no appreciation and consequently no growth.

Leo was much more interested in growing his money than preserving it. He had other accounts for wealth preservation. I'll never forget one day when the market abruptly plunged and he called me and said, "Frank, tell those amateurs to get out of the way, I'm coming in." And then he bought more stock.

This pattern played itself out repeatedly over the course of our relationship. Again and again, he demonstrated to me the freedom and peace of mind that come from having lived a life and managed his funds in such a way that in his golden years he could live life on his own terms. Leo exemplified the old school concept of buying low, holding tight, and never selling yourself short. That was his philosophy of investing and his philosophy of living.

I had the privilege of attending Leo's 100th birthday party at his granddaughter's home in Palos Verdes, where he laughed and danced and was full of life, even as a newly minted centenarian. He lived a long, full, happy, and healthy life, and when he passed away in 2004, his account was very substantial—my largest investment account by far at that point. He was my only client who made the bulk of his money by investing in the stock market, and he did it with joy in his heart and a complete absence of fear.

Imagine, Leo purchased his first stock directly from A. P. Giannini who was the founder of Bank of America way back when he still lived in San Jose! From that point forward, Leo continued buying Bank of America whenever it was down. I found it interesting that when Bank of America increased their dividend, Leo earned around $300,000 more per year than he had previously. Yet he really wanted the bank to keep the dividend the same and to plow the earnings back into the company to hopefully increase the earnings, thus increasing the value of the stock.

So, you might ask, what made Leo so successful? I think it was his discipline and courage to buy when the market was trading lower, particularly when it was trading a lot lower. That requires a strong belief that there will be better markets in the future. In other words, it takes optimism and confidence. You only get that kind of optimism and confidence when you know that—no matter what—your nut will be covered and you will be okay. Leo could hang in there and did not have to panic or sell, even when the markets were performing horribly.

And one last thing—Leo only bought companies that were well established and earning a good profit. He did his due diligence and understood what he was buying. Obviously, it takes more than that to be a whiz at investing in the stock market, but Leo's investment philosophy provides a solid foundation we can all learn from.

He achieved his success the old-fashioned way. He had been a moderate, balanced person his whole life. He built a lucrative practice as a dentist and, even though it wasn't his dream career, he stuck with it. He had a nice, comfortable house—he didn't build a palace. He understood his risk threshold and never exceeded it. And when he began his investment career in the second half of his life, he followed those same fundamentals that had carried him comfortably through the first half. He bought low and he held on—no matter the headwinds—and never sold himself short.

Debunking Common Myths About Rich People

Let's talk a little bit about the misconceptions we have about the wealthy, because if you want to be prosperous, you need to make friends with prosperity and understand a little something about wealthy people. Right off the bat, there are four myths about rich people that I want to debunk for you because they are false and can cloud your thinking about what you are trying to achieve in life.

False Myth #1: Rich People Are Horrible

Somehow or other, a belief persists that success and the affluence that comes with it is wrong or evil and wealthy people must be corrupt. Nothing could be further from the truth. First, you can't generalize about people—and that includes the wealthy. I have worked with very wealthy people in Orange County and they were *all* exemplary citizens. Good people are good people regardless of their financial worth and it's not a good idea to despise the thing we want to become. There is nothing evil about working hard, managing your money well, and winding up successful and comfortable.

False Myth #2: Rich People Are Just Lucky

Prosperity does not depend upon luck. You need to have a game plan in place to achieve prosperity. Just as the odds of winning the lottery are insanely small, so are the odds of getting rich through pure luck. You need to create and execute a plan to achieve the prosperous lifestyle you desire. You can't wait for your ship to come in—you need to steer that big boat into harbor through sound judgment and good financial planning.

False Myth #3: Money Is the Root of All Evil

Money in and of itself is not evil—what is evil is what some people choose to do with their wealth or the dishonest things they do to acquire wealth. If you pursue a goal of acquiring wealth honestly and ethically, your money will also be honest and ethical. Conversely, you will never, ever, be prosperous if you cheat to get ahead. Wealthy people who use their money to make the world a better place for everyone have funded most of the advances in society, including our greatest works of art.

So, money may be the root of some evil, but it is also the root of much good and many masterpieces.

False Myth #4: The Rich Don't Pay "Their Fair Share" of Taxes

This one really bugs me! Every April and October, my clients would call and move huge sums of money to their checking account to pay their taxes. It was depressing for me, let alone for them! Believe me, the rich pay an exorbitant amount of money in taxes. Nobody is getting a free lunch because they're wealthy.

I realize this is a bit of a political hot potato, but let's look at California as an example. If you earn $5 million, you will find yourself in a 37% federal tax bracket[5] and a 14.4% California tax bracket[6]—combined that is over 50%. In addition, when you pass away and your estate is valued at over $27.22 million, any dollar over that is hit with a federal estate tax of 40%.[7] Really, is that not enough? In addition, the top 1% of earners in California pay nearly 50% of all the tax revenue realized by the state of California.[8] So, as you can see, the rich do pay *a lot* of taxes—in California for sure, but in other states as well.

I have had the privilege of working with many wealthy people in my career, so I have learned a thing or two about what affluence looks like. Are successful, wealthy people always kind, polite, generous, and virtuous? Of course not. Sometimes they're a real pain in the neck, short sighted, and cheap, just as all of us can be. But the

---

5 Alex Durante, "2024 Tax Brackets," Tax Foundation, November 9, 2023, https://taxfoundation.org/data/all/federal/2024-tax-brackets/.

6 Robert W. Wood, "California 'Tax Break' Is 14.4% Tax on Earnings, 13.3% on Capital Gain," *Forbes*, January 8, 2024, https://www.forbes.com/sites/robertwood/2024/01/08/california-tax-break-is-144-tax-on-earnings-133-on-capital-gain/.

7 Amelia Josephson, "A Guide to the Federal Estate Tax for 2024," SmartAsset, last modified May 22, 2024, https://smartasset.com/taxes/all-about-the-estate-tax.

8 "Revenue Estimates," Governor's Budget Summary, accessed September 27, 2024, https://ebudget.ca.gov/2022-23/pdf/BudgetSummary/RevenueEstimates.pdf.

highly successful people I've met—the ones who earned it the hard way—do share some admirable qualities I've tried to cultivate in my own life. Use these building blocks as a guide to success in your own life.

The Building Blocks of a Prosperity Mindset

Ambition and Drive

To say successful people are ambitious and driven is an understatement. In my experience, successful people who start their own business often work 80 to 100 hours a week.[9] And in the very beginning, they have no downtime at all. They are fueled by their ambition to build something great and see their dream made real, and that takes tireless drive. I don't think the average person in America has a clue about how hard these entrepreneurs work to achieve their success. They possess boundless energy and are willing and eager to do the work required to be successful.

Intelligence and Street Smarts

I have always believed intelligence comes in two forms. First, there is street smarts, or what I call savvy. This means you can learn as you go and figure things out on the ground—in the real world—as you live your life. Secondly, there is intellectual knowledge, meaning you got an education, did well in school, and have an incredible ability to understand difficult concepts. I have found that when it comes to being successful with money, you should cultivate both forms of

[9] Kathleen Elkins, "Self-Made Millionaires Agree on How Many Hours You Should Be Working to Succeed," CNBC Make It, June 15, 2017, https://www.cnbc.com/2017/06/15/self-made-millionaires-agree-on-how-many-hours-you-should-be-working.html.

intelligence.

Visionary

Successful people are visionary. They have long vision. They can see far down the road and realize that big ideas—big dreams—take time to implement. They see problems or pain points as opportunities and understand the implications of their decisions down the line. They can see a problem, find a solution, and then execute on that vision with the ultimate result in mind. It's almost like they have a crystal ball and can look into the future and predict how their plan will change the world. This is an amazing ability and if you have it, nurture it! If you can imagine a better way, move on those instincts.

Generosity

Adopt the approach of making everyone you encounter feel better for having run into you. This can take many forms: being sincerely happy to see somebody, showing interest, and really listening to the people you meet makes everybody feel better.

I remember being at the Ronald Reagan Presidential Library and Museum in Simi Valley, California. I viewed a video presentation from the video archives. In the presentation, James Baker, Reagan's chief of staff, said one of the reasons Reagan was so successful was his ability to make everyone around him feel good. So, be like Ronald Reagan, be kind, be thoughtful, be interested, make people feel good when you're around, and you will be rewarded tenfold.

Prosperity and success are about more than being the richest person in the room. Prosperity means being the happiest person in the room because you've made everybody else around you happier just for knowing you. Prosperity is a happy family, a happy marriage, great relationships with your friends and colleagues—a supportive community you also support in kind. After all, what good is prosperity if you can't share and enjoy it with your loved ones and the world around you?

I worked with two sisters who were among the most incredible clients I've ever known. They exemplified the concept of generosity. They used their money like manure, as Dolly Levi famously said, and spread it around to make little things grow.[10] They gave a portion of their bond portfolios to at least 10 people. And the beauty of this gesture was that those 10 people who really needed it now had tax-free income. These two ladies also contributed to many worthwhile nonprofit organizations and used their prosperity to make their corner of the world a little better.

Bear in mind that giving isn't limited to monetary contributions—it can be your time, expertise, talent, wisdom, and guidance. Volunteering makes everybody's life richer. There are so many people and organizations that could use some help—it should not be too hard to find them.

You are only truly prosperous when you can give back to society. When you give, you will ultimately receive. Bread cast upon the waters returns a hundred-fold. Keep that thought with you as you go forward in life because it is one of the most powerful concepts we as humans can embrace. Believe me, there is far more joy in giving than receiving. I firmly believe the more you contribute, the richer you become.

Initiative and Confidence

The fact that you're reading this book indicates to me that you have already taken the initiative to learn how to achieve success. Now you must gain the confidence to keep going and develop a plan that will ultimately make your dreams a reality. Each step will inform the next

[10] Thornton Wilder, *The Matchmaker*, act 4 (New York: Samuel French, 1954).

until you reach your destination—the retirement of your dreams. *That* is the ultimate goal! You don't have to become a billionaire to be comfortable and free from worry about how to meet your financial obligations and maintain the lifestyle of your choice.

Courage and Gumption

When you invest your money, you put those funds at risk and there is no government guarantee that backs those funds. In other words, there is no safety net that will bail you out if your investments do not work out. No matter how soundly you invest, even if you follow every rule and tip in this book, you will still experience fluctuation in the market value of those investments.

You will need courage and gumption to weather the highs and lows. But rest assured that for the most part—if you have made sound investments—the fluctuation over time should be in an upward trajectory and those funds should grow into a very nice nest egg for you and your family. It takes courage to hold on when your account value drops and not to panic and sell out before your investments have the chance to recover. Remember that every time the market has gone substantially lower, it has *always* come back and moved to even higher highs!

Profiles in Courage

I met Susie and her husband in 1992. We became neighbors when they purchased a new home in our neighborhood, and eventually we became friends. Both Susie and her husband were extremely intelligent, had big vibrant personalities, and were extremely hard workers. Susie really took the bull by the horns when it came to putting their hard-earned money to good work. Boy was she courageous.

I will never forget that during the Great Recession of 2008–2009, when nobody had any confidence in *any* type of investment, Susie would call to tell me that hard times were the best times to invest. "There's blood in the streets and *now* is the time to buy," was her mantra. Sound familiar? She shared Leo's "damn the torpedoes" spirit because she could. Susie invested in California General Obligation (GO) bonds, paying more than 6% at that time. The benefit for her was that the interest was completely free of both state and federal taxes. She felt confident the state of California would meet their obligations and she did not have to worry.

California's constitution specifies school funding as the top repayment priority, and bondholders are a close second. Additionally, the constitution makes clear that the state cannot default on its obligations. The general obligation portion of the bond means the bonds are voter approved. Should it be necessary, the state can and will impose tax increases to pay the bondholders.[11] Seemingly, Susie could not lose. She was shrewd enough to recognize that and had the financial agility to act on the opportunity.

Looking back, even with those strong guarantees, there was still a huge amount of reluctance for investors to invest in California bonds—or anything else for that matter—during that grim time. But Susie had faith in California and faith in the fact things would improve over time. And Susie was right!

---

11 "Fitch Affirms California Infrastructure Bank's State School Fund Bonds at 'BBB+'; Outlook Positive," Fitch Ratings, July 18, 2013, https://www.fitchratings.com/research/us-public-finance/fitch-affirms-california-infrastructure-bank-state-school-fund-bonds-at-bbb-outlook-positive-18-07-2013; "Proposition 98," California Department of Education, last modified August 30, 2024, https://www.cde.ca.gov/ta/ac/sa/prop98.asp; Jonathan Kaplan and Scott Graves, "Guide to School Funding and the State Budget Process," California Budget & Policy Center, December 2022, https://calbudgetcenter.org/resources/california-school-funding-state-budget-process/.

Leo's Golden Rules

To sum up the focus this chapter, let's return to the philosophy of my dear friend Leo Arena, the best buy-and-hold investor I ever met. I urge you to study his golden rules below and incorporate them into your investment philosophy. I will end each of the next 11 chapters with "Golden Strategies" that provide insight and education on the many complexities of the investment world.

1. When the market is down, *buy.*
2. Once you buy, *hold.*
3. When the stock price plunges, *buy more.*
4. Be moderate with your money and your lifestyle.
5. Live within your means.
6. Know your risk tolerance and don't exceed it.
7. Scared money never wins. Invest with confident money.
8. Stay engaged with something you are passionate about.
9. Never sell yourself short and always have backup.

Workshop Topic

This chapter has one key concept—developing a prosperity mindset. Your assignment is to reach out to someone you know who is successful and ask them what they have done to achieve that success.

Prosperous people who have made their dream of success come true can be very inspiring. They have wisdom. You will be amazed at what they will share with you that might help you along your journey. Ask them about what they do for a living, how they prioritize savings, and which investment methods and/or advisors worked best for them. This will provide you with a solid foundation for building your version of financial success. Don't be afraid to ask questions—successful people love to share stories about how they made their dreams come true. And don't be intimidated! Affluent people have been kind and helpful to me throughout my career and I have no doubt they will be helpful to you as well.

Shareholder valued

One of the largest individual shareholders of Bank of America stock recently celebrated his 100th birthday in Palos Verdes, Calif. Frank Buchholz, senior investment officer (left), and John Chamberlin, Private Bank relationship manager (right), were on hand to help celebrate Dr. Leo Arena's (center) century mark. Arena received letters from Chairman and CEO Ken Lewis and President George Bush marking the occasion. Arena purchased his first share of bank stock directly from A.P. Giannini, founder of predecessor Bank of Italy, in 1918, and his birthday cake read, "1918 — Bullish on Bank of America."

08/20/2001

GOLDEN RULE 2

PAY YOURSELF FIRST

Understanding the True Value of a Dollar

I was a wealth manager, so by the time most people got to me they most likely were already successful in their pursuits in life and had amassed their fortune. They generally wanted me to help them preserve those assets not only for themselves but for their children and their children's children. They often were also looking for ways to give back some of their wealth in support of the causes that mattered most to them. In this way, they could be assured they were leaving a positive legacy.

In my 40+ years in the business, I found that people who earned their money the hard way by going to work every day, exercising self-discipline, and practicing sound financial hygiene throughout the course of their lives—the folks who had learned the value of a dollar—wound up better off financially in the long run. I believe this is because they understood that every dollar counted, no matter how much money they had in the bank. They had respect for their money and what it took to earn and build their fortune.

I have also had clients—often the children, grandchildren, or spouses of wealthy men or women—who have become accustomed to a certain lifestyle and haven't had to work for their privilege. In my experience, it is these people—the ones who don't understand the value of a dollar—that have a harder time holding on to their money. Even though these folks inherit millions, they have little to no regard for their wealth and often wind up losing it in the short run. They have never learned the fundamentals of sound financial self-care and often confuse the idea of paying themselves first with overspending and indulging on their every whim.

I remember one lovely lady in particular—the widow of a valued client of mine who inherited about $15 million when her husband passed away. After a period of mourning and making her way through the mountain of paperwork that inevitably follows the death of a loved one with assets, she immediately hit the designer floor at Bergdorf's. And I don't think she ever left. By the time I started paying attention, she was putting close to $100 grand a month on her credit cards, and most of the charges were, of course, at her favorite retail palace—the beautiful, irresistible, and exceedingly pricey Bergdorf's.

I knew we had a problem, so I asked her out to lunch. She suggested we meet at Bergdorf's, where else? I met her there and instantly recognized the seriousness of the problem when every single person who worked there knew her on a first-name basis. I gently tried to explain to this lovely lady—over a $40 salade niçoise—that if she kept spending at her current levels, she would soon go through all her money and have nothing but an over-stuffed closet full of more clothes than she could wear in one lifetime to show for it.

Of course, my cautionary guidance went in one ear and out the other. Her shopping impulse was obviously beyond the power of a financial advisor to address. Eventually, when the bills kept mounting and the bank balance kept shrinking, she had to sell her home and move to one in a cheaper housing market where there was no

Bergdorf's. After that, mercifully, things levelled out before she had run through all her inherited fortune.

The reason I share this story is to illustrate that taking care of yourself financially—making yourself your first priority—does not mean blowing $100 grand at Bergdorf's every month, or buying the latest spring Birkin bag, or obtaining a beach cottage in the Hamptons, unless you can actually and comfortably afford these purchases. No matter how good the splurge feels in the moment, real financial self-care means enjoying your money in the short term without risking your comfort and security over the long term. It means spending wisely and saving prudently.

Here are the four principles of good financial self-care you should bear in mind whenever money comes through the door.

The Golden Guide to Paying Yourself First

1. **Set up a retirement plan** (even if you're still in your twenties) and maximize your contributions as much as you can. I know it can be hard in the beginning, but do what you can and, more importantly, stick with it. The government has offered several very good ways to save for retirement. These include IRAs, 401(k)s and various pension accounts. Utilize these great programs available to you.
2. **Establish an emergency fund** and contribute to it until you have a half-year's income saved up for a rainy day. You never know when the next curveball will come at you, so make sure you have liquid funds set aside just in case you need them at a moment's notice.
3. **Contribute to an investment account with the help of a financial advisor.** This should only be money you can put at risk. Investment money should be money you do not need to

access. If the market goes down, you will be able to ride out the slump and allow your funds to recover when the market goes back up. Contribute regularly to this account, even if it is a small amount.

4. **Set up a discretionary account.** This is the fun money you can afford to spend on a splurge. And when you splurge, splurge on something that brings you maximum enjoyment. Reward yourself! It's good to enjoy the fruits of your labor but try not to forget about tomorrow while you are having fun today.

It's critical to start saving for retirement, especially when you're young.

People don't like to think about retirement, especially when they are just beginning their professional lives. Setting aside retirement funds, however, is a critical investment in your future and provides amazing tax benefits if you can train yourself early to start growing your savings. Young people have the longest time horizon and stand to gain the most benefit from their retirement savings. Retirement plans in America offer an incredible opportunity for young people to grow funds that are tax-deferred.

Here is a rundown of the various retirement plans available to you today.

A 401(k) Plan

This is a retirement plan offered by your employer. Its major benefit is that contributions are made on a pretax basis and the money grows tax-deferred until it's withdrawn. When the withdrawals take place, those funds are fully taxable.

The origins of the 401(k) date back to when Congress passed

the Revenue Act of 1978. In 1979, a gentleman by the name of Ted Benna noticed that the rules of the Revenue Act of 1978 made it possible for employers to establish a simple retirement program for their employees. It was Benna's interpretation of the 401(k) section within the Act that led to the creation of the first 401(k) for his own employees.[12]

Today, there is approximately $7.4 trillion invested in 401(k) plans with approximately 70 million participants.[13] Some 98% of employers offer the plan to their employees[14] of which around 68% are eligible to participate. Sadly, only 51% participate in contributing to their 401(k)[15] and only 14% make the maximum contribution.[16] If you can participate in a 401(k) through your employer, I would urge you to take advantage of that opportunity. Sadly, 50% of Americans retire today with no money saved.[17]

Another good reason to contribute to a 401(k) is that many companies offer an employer match. You can have your contributions automatically deducted from your payroll check and they will be taken

---

12 Sandra Block, "Meet the Architect of the 401(k) Plan," Kiplinger, December 21, 2021, https://www.kiplinger.com/retirement/retirement-plans/401ks/603971/meet-the-architect-of-the-401k-plan.

13 "401(k) Resource Center," Investment Company Institute, accessed September 27, 2024, https://www.ici.org/401k.

14 Elizabeth Gravier, "A 401(k) Match Is Like Free Money—Here's How It Works," CNBC, March 24, 2024, https://www.cnbc.com/select/401k-employer-match/.

15 "68 Percent of Private Industry Workers Had Access to Retirement Plans in 2021," U.S. Bureau of Labor Statistics, November 1, 2021, https://www.bls.gov/opub/ted/2021/68-percent-of-private-industry-workers-had-access-to-retirement-plans-in-2021.htm.

16 Sandra Block, "You May Have to Put Catch-Up Contributions in a Roth 401(k): That's Not a Bad Idea," Kiplinger, October 31, 2023, https://www.kiplinger.com/taxes/you-may-have-to-put-catch-up-contributions-in-a-roth-401k.

17 "Nearly Half of American Households Have No Retirement Savings," USA Facts, last modified November 9, 2023, https://usafacts.org/data-projects/retirement-savings.

out on a pre tax basis. The annual contribution limit is $23,000 or—if you are 50 years or older—$30,500.[18]

The advent of the 401(k) allowed many people who have no clue about investing to become investors. Once you start contributing, you are given a list of investment options that typically include stock and bond mutual funds and money market accounts, and you are asked to make a decision that will ultimately prove either very beneficial or not so much. Study the investment options carefully and learn from my advice. I was very fortunate to have made the correct decisions when it came to investing in my 401(k) and I know you can benefit from my experience.

Investment Options and Strategies for Your Retirement Funds

In my own 401(k), we were offered a wide variety of mutual funds to choose from. These included both stock and bond mutual funds as well as stable value money market accounts. More recently, exchange-traded funds (ETFs) have been added to the investment menu. These are like mutual funds in that you invest in a basketful of securities. Most often they would include stocks, bonds, or a combination of both. Listed below are fund types you may want to consider.

- **Value Fund**

  This fund would typically be composed of large companies that pay a dividend. This is the most conservative way to invest in the stock market.

- **Growth Fund**

[18] Claire Boyte-White, "How 401(k) Matching Works," Investopedia, last modified August 26, 2024, https://www.investopedia.com/articles/personal-finance/112315/how-401k-matching-works.asp.

This fund could be composed of large, medium, and small companies with a penchant for growing earnings over time in a significant way. Another way to look at growth stocks is that a company plows all earnings back into the company in an effort to grow revenue. These are most often newer companies that are not yet well established. The caveat is that these types of investments will fluctuate more than value-oriented companies will.

- **Bond Fund**

  This type of fund could include treasury and/or corporate bonds—both investment grade and high yield—and is more conservative than either of the two equity (stock) funds mentioned above. This is because, when investing in bonds either directly or through funds, you are lending money and receiving interest, not growth.

- **Target-Date Fund**

  This type of fund is much more aggressive. While you're young, a target-date fund will invest all your funds in stocks. Then, as you get closer to retirement, the asset mix in your portfolio automatically changes from equities to bonds which incur less risk. I never liked this type of fund—I found that as I got closer to retirement, yields on bonds had gotten so low that I could do better by keeping my funds in the stock market.

If I were 35 years old today and knew what I know now—after you read this book—I would split my investments and put 50% into large-cap growth stocks and 50% in large-cap value stocks. Given that I would probably retire at 65, this would give me 30 years to allow my funds to grow.

A Word to the Wise

As a side note, I would avoid buying the stock of the company you work for unless you feel very strongly about the prospects. Doing so tends to minimize your diversification. And, if the company you work for has financial problems, it can severely hurt the returns on your 401(k). Additionally, avoid borrowing against your 401(k). Treat it as if those funds are in a lockbox and cannot be accessed until you retire. Once you break that seal, it's so much easier to break it a second time and a third.

What Happens to My Money When I Retire?

When you retire, you will have the option of doing a rollover (transfer) to an IRA with an investment firm or keeping your IRA with your former employer. But *do not* cash out your 401(k), take the money, and run. First, you will be taxed, and second, if you are under 59½ years old you will pay a 10% early withdrawal penalty.[19] In my experience, I felt it best for clients to do an IRA rollover.

The major advantage to rolling over your 401(k) to an IRA—or in layman's terms, transferring it to your IRA account—is that you will have a vast menu of investment choices. You can have a separate managed account and buy individual treasuries, corporate bonds, and so on. With the 401(k) you're limited to mutual funds and ETFs which doesn't leave you with many choices or flexibility in your investment decision process. The other advantage of the IRA is you will now have a financial advisor working with you to assist in making those investment choices.

19 "IRA FAQs – Distributions (Withdrawals)," IRS, July 30, 2024, https://www.irs.gov/retirement-plans/retirement-plans-faqs-regarding-iras-distributions-withdrawals.

Investor beware! There are instances where people have rolled over their 401(k) into an IRA and the funds were not reinvested. Your funds need to be invested, or you will lose out. If this happens to you, transfer your account to another institution as your current provider is completely worthless!

Required Minimum Distribution (RMD)

The government requires you to start withdrawing funds from your 401(k) or your IRA account when you turn 73. To put it another way, this is the government's way of ultimately receiving taxes on your IRA. The percentage starts at approximately 5% and as you get older it increases every year. This is based upon the value of your IRA or 401(k) as of December 31 of the previous year end.[20]

If necessary, you can certainly take out more than the minimum distribution required. In my world, we could set up an account whereby a client receives monthly income and has taxes withdrawn as well. This makes it extremely convenient for the client and we would continuously monitor their portfolios and keep them on track.

IRA

An IRA, also known as an individual retirement account, is another terrific way to build your net worth either on a tax-deferred or tax-free basis. An IRA is nothing more than an investment account in which you can buy investments like stocks, bonds, mutual funds, etc. The best part is the government gives you some very beneficial tax treatments for both kinds of IRAs. The two types are explained

[20] "Retirement Plan and IRA Required Minimum Distributions FAQs," IRS, August 19, 2024, https://www.irs.gov/retirement-plans/retirement-plan-and-ira-required-minimum-distributions-faqs.

below.

1. **Traditional IRA**
   This is a type of retirement account that allows you to take a tax deduction for the amount you contribute to your IRA and allows you to grow the money on a tax-deferred basis. The funds are not taxable until they are withdrawn. When the funds are withdrawn, they are taxed at both the federal and state levels (assuming you live in a state that has a state income tax).
2. **Roth IRA**
   Roth IRAs differ from traditional IRAs in that the contributions are made with after-tax dollars. When your funds are withdrawn, they are tax free. In other words, all the potential gains or interest you have earned in your Roth IRA are nontaxable when withdrawn. To me, the Roth IRA is a far superior retirement plan than the traditional IRA. The tax-free withdrawals are worth far more than the deductibility of the contribution for the traditional IRA. And on top of that, you can earn a lot more money and still contribute to a Roth IRA.

Contribution Amounts

As of this writing in 2024, you can contribute up to $7,000 annually to a traditional or Roth IRA. If you are 50 years or older you can contribute $8,000.[21] There are many limitations surrounding the amount you can contribute as well as to the deductibility of the contribution, so check with your advisor. For example, you can only contribute as much as you have earned in a single year. In other words, if you earn $4,000 you are limited to contributing only $4,000 to your

[21] "Traditional and Roth IRAs," IRS, August 20, 2024, https://www.irs.gov/retirement-plans/traditional-and-roth-iras.

IRA. Also, you cannot contribute the maximum amount to both a traditional IRA and a Roth IRA.[22]

Remember that the contributions to a traditional IRA are tax deductible while the contributions to a Roth IRA are not.[23] Interestingly, if you're married, you can deduct any contribution to a traditional IRA if your joint income does not exceed $123,000.[24] However, with a Roth IRA you cannot deduct your contribution from your taxes. You are allowed to contribute if your joint income does not exceed $240,000.[25]

Other Retirement Plan Options

- **The SEP-IRA**

  We used to call these self-employed IRAs, but the actual name is Simplified Employee Pension IRAs. One of the major benefits of this type of retirement plan is the high contribution rate. For 2024, the contribution limit is 25% of net self-employment earnings or up to $69,000—whichever is less. Self-employed people can contribute to a SEP-IRA but need to make contributions to all employees at the same fixed percentage of employee pay. What that means is if you

22 "How Much Can I Contribute to My IRA Account This Year?," Guideline, accessed September 28, 2024, https://help.guideline.com/en/articles/8640552-how-much-can-i-contribute-to-my-ira-account-this-year.

23 "Topic No. 451, Individual Retirement Arrangements (IRAs)," IRS, September 20, 2024, https://www.irs.gov/taxtopics/tc451.

24 Katelyn Peters, "Traditional IRA Deductibility Limits," Investopedia, last modified September 5, 2024, https://www.investopedia.com/articles/retirement/03/011603.asp.

25 "Amount of Roth IRA Contributions That You Can Make in 2024," IRS, September 10, 2024, https://www.irs.gov/retirement-plans/plan-participant-employee/amount-of-roth-ira-contributions-that-you-can-make-for-2024.

contribute 10% of your compensation to your SEP-IRA, you must do the same for all employees. Remember the contributions to these plans are made only by the employer.[26]

- **Simple IRA (Savings Incentive Match Plan for Employees)**

  Both employees and employers can contribute to an individual's Simple IRA. You're eligible for a Simple IRA as a self-employed worker if you have fewer than 100 employees working for you. Employee contributions can be as much as $16,000 in 2024. If your salary is less than $16,000 you can contribute the entire amount you earn into a Simple IRA. If you are 50 years or older, you can contribute an additional $3,500.[27]

- **Profit Sharing Plans**

  The beauty of a profit-sharing plan is that it gives workers a share of the company's profits either quarterly or annually. Another benefit is businesses of any size can contribute to a profit-sharing plan. Only employers can contribute to profit-sharing plans. Employer contributions are established with a maximum contribution of $69,000 in 2024. For those who are 50 years or older, there is a catch-up provision of $3,500. Another thing to bear in mind is the contribution cannot be more than 25% of your total compensation.[28]

- **Money Purchase Plans**

  There are two distinct differences between money purchase

---

26 "SEP IRA Contribution Limits for 2024," Fidelity, June 20, 2024, https://www.fidelity.com/learning-center/smart-money/sep-ira-contribution-limits.

27 "Simple IRA Plan," IRS, last modified August 26, 2024, https://www.irs.gov/retirement-plans/plan-sponsor/simple-ira-plan.

28 "Choosing a Retirement Plan: Profit Sharing Plan," IRS, last modified August 19, 2024, https://www.irs.gov/retirement-plans/choosing-a-retirement-plan-profit-sharing-plan.

plans and profit-sharing plans. First, in a money purchase plan, employers are required to contribute for plan participants. Secondly, the contributions are not variable based upon the company's profitability. As an employer, you must establish a contribution rate. For 2024, the contribution rate is 25% of your compensation up to a maximum of $69,000. Only employers can contribute to a money purchase plan.[29]

All the above contribution limits are from 2024. You should consult with your financial advisor or check on the internet for current allowable contributions, as they do change.

Investment Options

The four retirement plans described above offer a little flexibility. They are typically opened as investment accounts with the help of a financial advisor, and they offer you a much broader menu of choices for placing your funds. You can invest in individual stocks and individual bonds. This contrasts with a 401(k) plan where you're limited to mutual funds and potentially ETFs.

Another advantage to these four retirement accounts is that as they grow in value, you can consider adding a separate money manager. For those of you investing in either a stock or a bond account, a separate managed account will increase your odds for getting a better return. In addition, you will not have to worry about capital gains and interest and dividends as these accounts all grow on a tax-deferred basis.

Any good financial self-care plan involves investing your funds in a retirement account. I would again urge you to invest as much as you comfortably can. Most of you will qualify to invest in a

---

[29] "Choosing a Retirement Plan: Money Purchase Plan," IRS, last modified August 19, 2024, https://www.irs.gov/retirement-plans/choosing-a-retirement-plan-money-purchase-plan.

retirement plan. Retirement plan contributions are made from your pay and can be deducted each time you are paid, so you don't have to worry about needing a large sum of money to get started.

Golden Strategies

1. Establish an emergency fund—and hands off until an emergency happens. (P.S. A sale at Neiman's does not constitute an emergency.) Contribute to it until you have a half-year's income saved up to help weather a financial storm or emergency.
2. Set up a retirement plan—even if you're still in your twenties—and maximize your contributions as much as possible. I know it can be hard in the beginning, but do what you can and stick with it.
3. As your resources grow, start contributing to an investment account with the help of a financial advisor. This should be money you can put at risk. Investment money should be money you don't need to access, so even if the market goes down, you will be able to ride out the slump and allow your funds to recover when the market goes back up.
4. Set up a discretionary account with fun money you can afford to spend or splurge. And when you splurge, buy something that brings you maximum enjoyment. It's good to enjoy the fruits of your labor, but try not to forget about tomorrow while you are having fun today.

Workshop Topics

1. I urge you to do a calculation using the following website: http://dqydj.com/sp-500-periodic-reinvestmen

t-calculator-dividends. This outstanding website allows you to go back in time and calculate what your total return would be based on a starting amount and funds added monthly from the Standard & Poor's 500 index. Of course, history is no guarantee of future returns, but it will give an indication as to what you could possibly grow your funds into.

2. Be sure to keep up to date with the allowable amounts of contributions for both IRAs and 401(k)s as they often change. This information is easily obtained on many websites.
3. Take the dollar amount you are looking for at retirement and multiply it by 5%. This will give you an indication of how much interest you might earn at retirement per year.
4. If you think that $1 million is enough to have saved at retirement, do some calculations surrounding the concept of inflation. If you are 35 now and want to retire at 65, assuming a 3% rate of inflation, you will need around $2,500,000 to achieve the same purchasing power today. *Yikes!* So, look ahead, count your pennies, and plan accordingly.

GOLDEN RULE 3

BUILD A STRONG FOUNDATION

The Keystones of Financial Security

I didn't get serious about investing until I entered the financial industry as a professional in 1982. At that time, I had truly little money to invest. I had a house payment, two car payments, and yes, even a payment to Beneficial Finance for our carpet, believe it or not.

When my wife and I married in 1980, we had a negative net worth. We owed $100,000 on our house that we paid $125,000 for and owed around $10,000 for our two Honda Accords and around $3,000 for our new carpet. A funny thing is that house today is worth over $1.5 million, and a similar Honda Accord today would probably cost well over $30,000. This shows what inflation does to your purchasing power. It also shows how your nest egg can grow over time. Just as prices increase, so does value.

The first investments we made were to our contributory IRAs—$2,000 a year for seven or eight years. I invested in my own IRA more aggressively and invested in my wife's more conservatively. I invested those funds into stock mutual funds. Today, those contributions are worth $226,000 for myself and $211,000 for my wife. This example clearly illustrates my thoughts about investing. For the long term, investing in stocks is the way to go and you can certainly see how a small sum of money can grow to a substantial sum over the long run.

In this chapter I will describe five investment instruments. This book provides guidance on all of them but primarily on stocks and bonds. The other three investment vehicles are real estate, commodities, and collectibles.

1. Stocks

My favorite form of investment is, without question, the stock market. This is probably because I have done well in the market and watched my clients do well. For myself, I had a long-term horizon when I started in the investment world, so most of my investments could be in stocks, which favor a long horizon. During the 40 years I was invested in the stock market, we had a very solid bull run with a few very notable exceptions.

Over my time in the financial services industry, I have watched people interact with their money and the market. One thing I can tell you for sure is the average person has no idea how the stock market works and investors make emotional decisions based on impulse, which can get them into a lot of trouble. I get it—the market is often perplexing and sometimes a complete conundrum. That's why there are people like me around to help. It's a good idea to leave financial strategy to a professional you can trust, but you still need to know what and how you are buying in the market.

Many people consider investing in the stock market to be the same as gambling. Nothing could be further from the truth. Investing is not at all like gambling—comparing the two is a false equivalency that can get you into trouble. Investing should never be a gamble but a strategic and calculated risk made in exchange for mostly predictable outcomes.

When you put your money down on a certain number on the roulette table, you are relying on pure luck because you can't investigate a number. That is gambling. When you are investing in the market, you are buying shares in a company. Companies have an identity, a track record, and financial statements. They are not just numbers on a wheel. You do your due diligence, investigate a business's financials, or use their products and services to judge for yourself if a company is providing value and likely to do well on a go-forward basis. You can get a feel for how well the company is performing over time and begin to assess whether they will be able to sustain growth over the long term.

Of course, there is always a degree of risk when you are investing in stocks, but if you remember the fundamentals as I've outlined them, you can eventually sit back and watch your money grow. Think of it like this—when you buy a stock, you are buying a small percentage of that company. So, for example, if you buy 10 shares of Microsoft, you will have a small percentage of ownership in Microsoft. What happens from that point is you will see the value of your ownership stake and the value of that stock fluctuate over time given any number of variables. You hold the stock or sell it based on the stock's performance and the advice of a solid investment advisor.

The Market by the Numbers

Market Capitalization

One of the most basic ways to check the valuation of stock is to look at the market capitalization, sometimes known as market cap. Market capitalization is defined by the number of shares outstanding multiplied by the current price of the stock. The five largest companies in America by market cap would be as follows: Apple $3.418

trillion, Microsoft $3.098 trillion, Nvidia $3.040 trillion, Alphabet $2.053 trillion, and Amazon $1.934 trillion.[30]

Market cap can be broken down into three categories: small-cap, mid-cap, and large-cap. Generally, the smaller and mid-cap stocks offer more growth potential—however, they also have more potential risk because they are not well established yet and have a greater chance of failure.

1. Large-cap stocks have a market cap of at least $10 billion.
2. Mid-cap stocks have a market cap of between $2 billion to $10 billion.
3. Small-cap stocks have a market cap of between $300 million to $2 billion.[31]

Dividend Yield

First off, what is a dividend? A dividend is a portion of earnings that is paid to a company's common shareholders. Most of the time, a dividend is paid in cash, but some corporations pay in stock. Dividends are usually issued quarterly but may be distributed monthly or, in the case of foreign corporations, annually. They are most often paid to reflect their financial stability and attract investors. Growth stocks don't pay dividends—examples include Amazon and Alphabet, which have never issued dividends.

Dividend yield is calculated by taking the dividend dollar amount and dividing it by the share price. Thus, if a stock is selling at $50 per share and pays a dividend of $2 per share, the dividend

---

30 "Largest American Companies by Market Capitalization," Companies MarketCap, last modified October 4, 2024, https://companiesmarketcap.com/usa/largest-companies-in-the-usa-by-market-cap/.

31 "How Well Do You Know Market Cap?," Charles Schwab, November 20, 2023, https://www.schwab.com/learn/story/how-well-do-you-know-market-cap.

yield is 4%. Bear in mind that the dividend dollar amount is variable and can be increased or decreased based on how well the corporation is performing. If you look at Bank of America for example, they were paying $0.64 per share per quarter as of July 2008. After the Great Recession, the dividend was cut to a penny per share per quarter. That took place in March 2009. Today the dividend has increased to $0.26 per share per quarter and, as of this writing on, October 21, 2024, the dividend yield is 2.49%.[32]

Price-Earnings Ratio (P/E)

The price-earnings ratio is also known as the P/E and is most often used for valuation purposes. It is defined by dividing the earnings-per-share into the price of the stock. It tells you how much you are paying for each dollar of earnings. This will give you some idea of the valuation of the stock as compared to its peers in the marketplace. High price-earnings ratios can be a sign that a stock is overvalued. This is particularly true in the technology sector. A company that is not earning money will not have a price-earnings ratio.[33]

To give some flavor, look at the P/E ratio of the following six stocks as of October 21, 2024:

- Bank of America: 15.13[34]
- J. P. Morgan: 12.4[35]

---

32 "Dividends for Bank of America (BOA) Upcoming Dividends," Bank of America, accessed September 28, 2024, https://investor.bankofamerica.com/shareholder-information/dividends.

33 Jason Fernando, "Price-to-Earnings (P/E) Ratio: Definition, Formula, and Examples," Investopedia, last modified July 30, 2024, https://www.investopedia.com/terms/p/price-earningsratio.asp.

34 "P/E Ratio for Bank of America (BAC)," Companies MarketCap, accessed October 2, 2024, https://companiesmarketcap.com/bank-of-america/pe-ratio/.

35 P"/E Ratio for JPMorgan Chase (JPM)," Companies MarketCap, accessed October 2, 2024, https://companiesmarketcap.com/jp-morgan-chase/pe-ratio/.

- Citigroup: 17.62[36]
- Apple: 36.01[37]
- Microsoft: 35.52[38]
- Nvidia 67.50[39]

Talk about disparity between bank stocks and technology stocks! The tech stocks are in a growth phase currently, while the bank stocks are more of a mature investment that will generate incremental but predictable growth over time. You probably will not see huge earnings growth from bank stocks as you would in tech stocks, but you have the reassurance that you will realize predictable growth and won't lose your shirt in a volatile market.

I am not trying to make you an expert in investing in the stock market. Rather I'm trying to provide you with a foundation of knowledge so you're better equipped to discuss your own situation with a qualified financial advisor and that person in the mirror who is responsible for making your dreams come true.

A Caveat

I would never encourage anyone who isn't a professional to invest in stocks by themself without guidance from a qualified expert. The market is complex and has a hair trigger at times, so an average investor is much better served by getting help from a professional management firm. They are better equipped to make investment

36 P"/E Ratio for Citigroup (C)," Companies MarketCap, accessed October 2, 2024, https://companiesmarketcap.com/citigroup/pe-ratio/.

37 "P/E Ratio for Apple (AAPL)," Companies MarketCap, accessed October 2, 2024, https://companiesmarketcap.com/apple/pe-ratio/.

38 "P/E Ratio for Microsoft (MSFT)," Companies MarketCap, accessed October 2, 2024, https://companiesmarketcap.com/microsoft/pe-ratio/.

39 "P/E ratio for NVIDIA (NVDA)," Companies MarketCap, accessed October 2, 2024, https://companiesmarketcap.com/nvidia/pe-ratio/.

decisions and provide ongoing oversight. You can't compete with a team of professionals who do this all day every day.

When it comes to picking which area or sector of the stock market you want to invest in, be advised that the large-cap dividend payers are the least risky. The smaller companies known as small-cap companies are the riskiest but also offer the most potential return. There is an inverse ratio in the money world between risk and reward. I strongly suggest that as you grow older, you invest in the large-cap dividend payers. Never jeopardize your principle.

Growth Versus Value

A growth stock is an instrument still in its growth stage. Growth stocks typically take all their earnings and plow them back into growing the company. A value stock is a stock inexpensive in relation to its peers—that could be based on several factors, including its price-earnings ratio. An example would be two large banks where one has a substantially lower P/E ratio than the other, meaning one is a "cheap" stock in comparison to its peer. A perfect example of a value stock would be Bank of America, which is tried, tested, and true. It has performed reliably over the course of time and will most likely continue to do the same. It is low risk.[40]

It is interesting to note that value investments outperform growth investments around 50% of the time. Growth beats value the other 50% of the time. As technology stocks have fallen into the growth category, growth stocks have outperformed value stocks and been the best-performing stocks for several years. A perfect example is Nvidia

---

40 "Growth vs. Value: Two Approaches to Stock Investing," Merrill, accessed September 28, 2024, https://www.merrilledge.com/article/growth-vs-value-investing-two-approaches-to-stocks.

which has gone up enormously.[41] I think it's advisable to still have some funds invested in both categories.

Balance Is Everything

A balanced portfolio is critical to long-term investment success. I strongly suggest rebalancing your portfolio on a yearly basis. It's not that complicated. Rebalancing just means you take some profits from the better performing categories and add them to the lower performing categories.

Rebalancing also entails capturing profits either by sector or geography and taking those funds to purchase poorer performing stocks at a less inflated price. While this is *not* a guarantee of better performance, it does enhance your odds. Another benefit is that you keep your portfolio in balance, meaning you do not have too much concentration in one space, which can serve to minimize risk.

What About Risk?

So many clients I have worked with over the years had a total aversion to investing in the stock market because of the risk involved. Many clients were fearful they could lose their entire nest egg and steered clear. So, let's talk about risk. First, don't be intimidated! Confront the threat of risk with an eye toward the long-term horizon. This does not mean forever, but I do strongly suggest giving the market at least five years to grow your funds. Also, these need to be funds you will not need to access within that time span.

Investing in the market requires that you have back up funds set aside for whatever cash needs may arise so you don't need to access your investment account. This will make it possible for you to endure

---

[41] Björn Jesch, "Value vs. Growth," DWS, accessed October 4, 2024, https://www.dws.com/en-us/insights/cio-view/macro/cio-special-03272024/.

fluctuations in the market. Back up funds ensure you won't have to sell stock to pay your bills, provide for emergencies, or buy a new car, a new house, or start a business. The longer your time horizon, the better your odds of getting greater returns from the stock market. If you have a looming tax bill or buying a new house or a Ferrari in the next six months, then I would avoid the stock market. There are better options for you.

Investing in the stock market can be like taking a plane to your next destination. Along the way, you will more than likely encounter some turbulence, but you can't jump out of the plane because it's a bumpy ride. You must sit on that plane all the way to your destination. In fact, your survival depends on it.

I remember all too well in 2009 when my 401(k) became a 1.8(k). I had lost a huge percentage of my retirement savings overnight. Those were some scary, scary times! But fortunately, I didn't need those funds at the time, so I could ride out the storm. Today my 401(k) has grown substantially from that sorry number in 2009 and, looking back, there is no doubt that if I did not invest those funds back into the stock market along the way—through good times and bad—the value would be half of what it is today.

What all this boils down to is that, historically, the stock market has produced positive returns for most reasonable investors. I personally have been a huge beneficiary of those returns, and you can be one as well.

Preferred Stocks

The main difference between common stock, which we have been discussing thus far, and preferred stock is that common stock affords you voting rights. This means as a shareholder you have greater say in the workings of the company you invested in. Preferred stock does not include your voice in decision-making. Another difference is preferred stocks often have a higher dividend yield in comparison to common stocks. Over time, common stocks may increase their dividends as earnings grow, which contrasts with preferred stocks that pay a fixed rate.

Preferred stocks typically pay a quarterly dividend. It is generally a fixed percentage and doesn't change with fluctuations in interest rates or the company's earnings. These types of stocks are what we refer to as perpetual, which means they have no maturity date.

Additionally, preferred stocks can be called away at the discretion of the issuer. Called away means the issuer pays you the face value of your shares—what is also referred to as "par"—and you no longer earn interest on that security. Par—unlike in golf—refers to the face value of the security. This is the amount you would receive at maturity or if the security was called by the issuer. Look at it like a $2 bill. The face value is $2, which is what you spend at your local retailer. However, if it was an older $2 bill and in perfect condition, it might be worth $10 to a collector.

The main advantage of preferred stock over common stock is the preferred shareholder has a greater claim to the company's assets and earnings in bankruptcy. And to be clear, in bankruptcy, bondholders have the greatest claim to assets. Companies, even big companies, do go belly up sometimes as most of us who have been around for a while have seen firsthand.

Finally, preferred stock is usually issued by corporations of lower credit quality.

Given the fact there is no maturity date, little upside, and plenty of downside, I do not recommend preferred stocks. The downside is if interest rates rise, the value of your preferred stock will drop. The loss can be substantial and may never return to the price you paid. Also, because preferred stocks are of lower credit quality, they're much more subject to market fluctuation, especially in down markets.

This was particularly true in June 2009 when investors lost all confidence in all investment products, especially those of lower credit quality. This even included real estate. My own home went down in value by approximately 25%! Also included were preferred and common stocks of poorer performing companies and their bonds. In general, there are better ways to earn income and less risky ones as well. Thus, I would never recommend buying preferred stock.

The Good, the Bad, and the Very Likely

I thought it would be helpful to present some perspective regarding the historical returns on three major stock market indexes. After you have read this section, the question you need to ask yourself is—can you handle the ups and downs of the stock market and still sleep well at night? This is called your risk tolerance. It's important to know where your boundaries lie so you do not exceed them and spend your time stressing out. The goal of financial security is peace of mind.

The Three Major Stock Market Indexes in America

1. ***Dow Jones Industrial Average***, sometimes known as the Dow or the DJIA, is composed of 30 prominent companies from the United States listed on the stock exchange. It is a price-weighted index.
2. ***Standard & Poor's 500***, also known as the S&P 500, tracks the performance of 500 large companies, again for the United States. This is a capitalization-weighted index.
3. ***NASDAQ 100***, often referred to as the NASDAQ, tracks 100 large American companies listed on the NASDAQ stock exchange.

Looking at the returns on these three major stock market indexes provides a great deal of information about their performance over the last many years. If you look at the performance over the last three years, five years, 10 years, and 15 years, the NASDAQ 100 has performed best in each of those time frames.[42] Now, if only it were that easy! If only all you had to do was buy NASDAQ 100 index stocks and live happily ever after. Unfortunately, it is not so straight forward and the statistics I am going to show you will prove that.

The NASDAQ 100 carries a significant technological component and as such is very susceptible to risks including innovation, economic turbulence, and higher interest rates. If on March 27, 2000, you invested $117,750 into the exchange-traded fund (ETF) QQQ, which tracks the NASDAQ 100 index, sadly by October 9, 2002, the value would have dropped to approximately $20,060. And, even if you continued to hold that ETF through thick and thin, by October 2024 you would have made slightly more than four times your original investment with an approximate return of just less than 6% per year. But that would have required holding this position for over 24 years. You have to ask yourself—would you have had the patience and fortitude to do that?

Granted, this is looking at something from an extreme point of view, but you need to understand that the NASDAQ 100 is by far the most volatile of the three indexes mentioned above. Remember to always, *always* diversify your portfolio. In this case that means buying stocks from different sectors including those in the Dow Jones Industrial Average and the S&P 500.

Red Flags

Some final words of caution. Even though the 15-year average return on the NASDAQ 100 index was 16.4%, the 15-year return on the

[42] Cory Mitchell, "Historical Average Returns for NASDAQ 100 Index (QQQ)," TradeThatSwing, September 11, 2024, https://tradethatswing.com/historical-average-returns-for-nasdaq-100-index-qqq/.

S&P 500 was 12.6% and the Dow Jones industrial average return was 10.7.[43] Be forewarned—the NASDAQ returns can and will be very volatile into the future. As an example, if you look at the returns of the three indexes for 2022, the Dow was down 8.78%, the S&P 500 was down 18.11% and the NASDAQ 100 was down a whopping 32.97%.[44]

It's these numbers that give people pause when it comes to investing in the stock market. The market is not a panacea—even though returns on the S&P 500 have averaged around 10% per year since the Great Depression[45] and are up three out of every four years, there is certainly no guarantee whatsoever your performance will be the same in the future.

So, you must ask yourself—can I handle the volatility? What is my risk tolerance threshold? And realistically, do I have enough years in front of me to recover when the market returns are poor like they were in 2022? If not, you would be well advised to invest a sizable percentage of your portfolio in bonds. They are certainly going to be less volatile than the stock market, but if you invested in bonds prior to 2022, you would have had a negative return on your bond portfolio in 2022 as well. There was no place to hide in 2022 except for short-term treasuries and money markets.

---

43 Trevor Jennewine, "Here's the Average Stock Market Return Over the Last 15 Years," Motley Fool, NASDAQ, June 27, 2024, https://www.nasdaq.com/articles/heres-average-stock-market-return-over-last-15-years.

44 Dan Caplinger, "Just How Badly Did Stock Markets Perform in 2022?," Motley Fool, NASDAQ, December 30, 2022, https://www.nasdaq.com/articles/just-how-badly-did-stock-markets-perform-in-2022.

45 Ian Webster, "Stock Market Returns Since 1929," Official Data Foundation, accessed September 28, 2024, https://www.officialdata.org/us/stocks/s-p-500/1929.

2. Bonds (not James Bond)

Bonds, sometimes known as fixed-income investments, are a way of lending money to a corporation or another entity. If you buy a bond from General Motors, you are lending money to them in the hope they will pay you interest on the instrument and the principal at maturity. Another way to look at the bond world is this is a debt instrument, as you do not have any ownership in the company or entity. I will provide you with more information on bonds in chapter 4.

3. Real Estate

Real estate has proven to be valuable for investors, particularly in places like Southern California where I live. Investing in real estate can take many forms, including commercial real estate, which is comprised primarily of industrial property and apartments but goes all the way through to your own personal residence. I have found that if you put in the time to manage your real estate property, you can do quite well in this investment area. But remember, there are three Ts when it comes to investing in real estate.

The first T is talent, which means you must have the talent to find the piece of real estate that has the potential to appreciate.

The second T means you need the temperament to manage real estate. Simply put, you need the temperament to evict people or businesses not paying their rent and so on.

And the last T is time. You need to have the time to manage real estate in the first place. You can hire professional management to assist you in this endeavor, but as many real estate investors will tell you, this is not as easy as it sounds. Good management is hard to find, and certainly, the first two Ts I mentioned still come into play. For these reasons, I did not invest in real estate except for my own home.

That being said, I do think you should look at your own home as an investment. The good news is it has the potential for price appreciation over the long run—sometimes even the short run—and you get the added benefit of investing in something you can live in and enjoy. The home we now live in is worth around three times more than we paid for it. Interestingly, considering we have owned it for 27 years, the return was not as good as if I had invested those same funds into the stock market over the same period. But am I happy with the return? Absolutely, because a home you're comfortable in and happy with is a priceless commodity.

I have had clients who made their living from investing in real estate, primarily commercial real estate, and used the rent for income. They used my services for short-term money management such as investing in money market instruments like Treasury Bills and bank CDs. I talked to many clients who were tearing their hair out over nonresponsive or unavailable management and/or difficult tenants. Property is manageable but sometimes the people involved are not.

4. Commodities

Commodities are material goods. Investing in commodities may take the form of buying corn futures, gold, silver, oil futures, and so on. This is a very risky form of investment. Often, you will borrow money to make an investment in this product category. Using leverage (meaning borrowing) for investing will magnify your gains or losses accordingly. Given the complex nature of these investments and the extremely substantial risk, I never chose to invest in commodities, and I would urge you to stay away as well unless you really know what you're doing and are passionate about the sector.

5. Collectibles

The final form of investment is collectibles. These take the form of buying fine art, watches, jewelry, antiques, vintage automobiles, or other items that fall into the collectible category. This again is something I chose not to do. If you have a keen interest in a certain type of collectible you would like to own—regardless of its resale value—go ahead and invest for the joy of collecting. You might make money upon resale but it's uncommon, and in my experience not a reliable revenue stream.

Which of These Investments Has the Best Return?

The answer to this critical and eternal question is based on the length of time and specific years of the investment. It may be hard to track, given the finite number of buys and sells of that particular investment. As an example, if you look at 2022, both stocks and bonds had negative returns. This was primarily because the Federal Reserve raised interest rates to combat inflation.

In doing research for this book, I came across a remarkably interesting chart from New York University. It shows the value of $100 invested at the start of 1928 and what happened on a year-by-year basis—both in terms of returns and valuations—from then until the end of 2023. The categories they chose were S&P 500, the three-month T-bill, the U.S. T-bond, the BAA corporate bond, and real estate.[46]

Bear in mind that real estate is the hardest investment to track

[46] "Historical Returns on Stocks, Bonds and Bills: 1928-2023," New York University Stern School of Business, January 2024, https://pages.stern.nyu.edu/~adamodar/New_Home_Page/datafile/histretSP.html.

given that returns are based on selling the asset, which does not take place every day like other categories do. Nevertheless, I found the information extremely intriguing and very thoughtfully presented. The $100 invested in the five categories grew to valuations as follows: S&P 500, $787,018; three-month T-bill, $2,249; U.S. T-bond, $7,278; BAA corporate bonds, $49,525; and real estate, $5,360. This is a graphic example of why I strongly believe investing in the stock market is prudent for so many investors. Since the Great Depression, stocks have outperformed every other investment by many multiples.

The S&P 500 has had an annualized return of 10.67% per year since its modern structure was instituted in 1957. If we go back to 1928, before the modern structure, S&P 500 returns averaged 10.22%. This is where the familiar quotation that "10% is the average return in the stock market" comes from. The irony, however, is that returns between 1926 and 2023 were in the band between 8% and 12% only seven times. The rest of the time returns were sometimes much lower but were usually much higher. Volatility will always remain in the stock market. Let's look at the returns from 1982 until the end of 2023.

- 30 years 1984–2023, 9.67%
- 20 years 2004–2023, 9%
- 10 years 2014–2023, 11.02%

I present these statistics to demonstrate why I believe the best investment for the average person is stocks over the long term. Yes, there will be volatility and some years even losses—however, the market is up approximately 70% of the time. This means for every 10 years, you will have seven years up and three down. Those are pretty good odds.

More importantly, if you look at the average return of 10%, your money will double every 7.2 years. This is based on the rule of 72, which states you can know how long it will take an investment to double by dividing 72 by the rate of return. If the 10% return continues, your money will double every 7.2 years. So, consider this—if you invest $100,000 today, it will potentially be worth $200,000 in 7.2 years. To carry the analogy further, it will potentially be worth $400,000 in 14.4 years, $800,000 in 21.6 years, and $1.6 million in 28.8 years.

You can see firsthand why experts believe investing in the stock market requires a long-term horizon. Some experts even go on to say long-term requires thinking in decades not just years. If you are in your thirties and lucky enough to be able to invest in a 401(k), I would *urge* you to consider investing most of your funds in the stock market!

The Bottom Line on the Bottom Line

Historically, without question, stocks have provided the best return, especially for the average investor. Although there will always be exceptions, dollar for dollar, over time, the bottom line is investing in the stock market offers the best potential outcome. The best way to invest in stocks is to do so with a professional money manager who does this with a team of astute investment professionals to offer you the best potential outcome.

You Should Own Stocks, Not Buy Stocks

There is a difference! Leave the buying to the professionals who do this 40+ hours a week, every week. They have a distinct advantage over you. You may be one of those people who has the talent and savvy to navigate the stock market with success, but you would be the exception rather than the rule. Do not overestimate your skills. Ego has no place in the world of wealth creation.

Golden Strategies

1. Get comfortable with the concept of investing in stocks. There is an old saying: "No guts, no glory." You need to take a risk to achieve. Garner the courage to put your feet in the water and invest in stocks, but only with money you can afford to put at risk.
2. For most people, investments should be handled in a professionally managed account—either a separately managed account or a mutual fund, which will be discussed later in this book. Having your funds managed professionally will increase the odds of getting a better return than if you try to do it yourself. Yes, you will pay a fee of somewhere between 1% and 2%, but if you can average close to 10% per year, that fee is well worth it.
3. Remember that no matter how you go about investing in the stock market, be sure you have a time horizon of five years or more. You will read this more than once in this book but investing in stocks is not—and never has been—a promising idea in the short run. If you will need funds in six months, never, ever put those funds in the stock market.
4. When it comes to the market, time is your best friend, but trying to time the market is your worst enemy!
5. The three things I find drive stock prices can be summed up in the letters E, I, and E—Earnings, Innovation, and Expectation. Pay attention to all three when doing your due diligence. Let me give you some examples of each. Companies with growing earnings include companies like Amazon and Costco. Companies with innovation include companies like Apple and Microsoft. And companies with expectation include companies like Tesla. I remember all too well when Tesla was losing money and the stock kept going

up. I thought, huh? This was a clear-cut example of investors buying the stock on the expectation Tesla would ultimately make money, and sure enough it did.

6. The best time to invest in the stock market is when it feels like the entire world is coming apart and you ask yourself, what the hell am I doing? This of course would be when the market has cratered and entering it can be super scary to say the least. The feeling can be summed up by saying, "Yeah, buy now, but it could certainly go lower." Look at it this way—if you are considering purchasing a home and the one you like just had the price lowered by $100,000, would you be more inclined or less inclined to buy it? Rhetorical question! Over the many years I've been in this crazy business, down markets have been the best time to invest. As the saying goes, "no guts, no glory."

Workshop Topics

1. Get familiar with the returns and volatility of the various market indexes. These include the three major indexes: the Dow Jones Industrial Average, the Standard & Poor's 500, and the NASDAQ. The question is, can you handle the increased volatility of the NASDAQ versus the S&P 500? Personally, over the very long run, I think the NASDAQ will probably perform best. However, if your start date was in 1999, you would not be saying that right now—but if you started in late 2001, you hit a grand slam.
2. Pick out your favorite publicly traded company. Publicly traded means the company has issued stock and is owned by the shareholders, whereas privately held means the company has not issued stock that trades on an exchange. Go to the company's website and look for their annual report. When

you skim the report, look for two distinct items: growth in sales (revenue) and growth in earnings. Having familiarity with just these two items will give you a comfort level and knowledge about the company you might invest in.

Look at all the ways in which a company is valued to educate yourself about the numbers you are looking at. This will not only help you better understand your investments but also reinforce the reasons why individual stock purchases are made by professionals. Educating yourself on how to value companies by familiarizing yourself with their annual reports will make you a smarter investor in the long run.

GOLDEN RULE 4

FIND A FINANCIAL ADVISOR YOU TRUST

How to Know When You've Found the Right Advisor for You

One of the most important relationships you will form in your life will be your choice of a financial advisor. I have seen what good advisers can do for a portfolio and, unfortunately, what can happen when things go bad. Choosing the right guidance is critical to your wealth creation.

I should say, right off the bat—and it might sound funny coming from a financial advisor—but I do not like most financial advisors. I have found many of them to be supremely arrogant and even condescending. And unfortunately, all too many financial advisors are strictly in it to make money and really do not care about their clients. Financial advisors come in all flavors—by that I mean that some are skilled, some are not, some look out for your best interests, but many do not. So, heads up!

When you start to shop for a financial advisor, you need to be aware of what you're up against and some insight as to how to go about picking an advisor who's right for you. Many financial advisors are not advisors at all, they're just financial salespeople. Their only goal is to try to make as much money from you as possible by selling you their financial product. A perfect example of this would be the financial advisor who only wants to sell you annuity products. Is it because annuity products are best for you, or because they are one of the highest producing commission products a financial advisor has in his or her toolbox?

Be aware that financial advisors are extremely skilled in the sales process. I am convinced that most successful financial advisors could sell snow to Alaskan residents. So, be forewarned when you start talking to financial advisors that you will be talking to some of the most skilled salespeople of any profession and, unfortunately, not all of them are looking out for your best interest.

Characteristics to Look for in a Financial Advisor

- **Honesty and Transparency**

  In my practice, I needed to be completely honest and transparent in discussing investments. My clients always appreciated this and you should appreciate it with your advisor too. You are hiring an advisor to tell you the truth and help you figure out the steps for handling your objective in the best way possible. If someone does not tell you the facts, you can't make informed decisions. When it comes to money, you don't want to be sold a bill of goods.

- **Patience**

  The problem with many financial advisors is they lack patience and can be condescending toward people who don't understand the nuances of the financial markets. Look for an advisor who is welcoming and patient, because this is critical for good financial management. You want someone who will take the time to listen, cares about what you have to say, and is willing to spend the time necessary to educate you about your investments. One thing I always told prospective clients was they could ask any questions, even "dumb ones," and I would provide an answer in more detail than they had asked for.

I remember one of my clients asking me about investing in an annuity. She was quite well off, lived in Beverly Hills, and was approximately 75 years old at the time. I told her she needed an annuity like she needed another hole in her head. She and I both laughed. Her next comment was that this was what she thought as well. If I had gone for the sale, she would have known I was advising against her best instincts. It was a trick question, and my answer let her know she could trust me. She provided me with a refreshing reminder that my clients were not born yesterday.

Pick an advisor who speaks to you as a peer and doesn't talk down to you or try to intimidate you with their thorough knowledge of a subject you know nothing about. I am always careful to remind my clients that I wasn't born with investment knowledge. I too have made my share of mistakes along the way. My goal was always to put my clients at ease and reassure them I was listening, I cared, I had been in their shoes, and they would receive my absolute best advice.

I would urge you to look for these characteristics when you are interviewing candidates for your financial advisor position. If they lack patience or do not seem to be totally honest, keep looking. This will not be your easiest task, but it will certainly make a dramatic difference in your investment results, so stick it out and choose carefully. You will thank me later.

At my first meeting with a prospective client, I would always tell them they were welcome to bring a confidant to the meeting. That person could be a friend, a relative, or one of their professional advisors like an attorney or CPA. I also told them they would not be asked to make any decisions at that first meeting and were welcome to ask me as many questions as they would like.

Financial Advisors Come in All Shapes, Sizes, and Species

1. Traditional Financial Advisors

I was a traditional financial advisor when I worked at Merrill Lynch. A traditional financial advisor works at a major firm such as Morgan Stanley, J. P. Morgan, UBS, and Edward Jones, and may be a certified financial planner (CFP) or hold another professional designation. CFP is an especially important title when it comes to financial planning. It requires passing rigorous and difficult courses in trust and estate planning, college tuition funding, debt consolidation, etc. At Merrill Lynch, our minimum account size was $250,000 and we offered a full array of financial planning, including trust and estate planning, personal wealth analysis, retirement analysis, and so on.

2. Registered Investment Advisors

A registered investment advisor (RIA) is part of a professional financial firm that offers advice on a fiduciary basis. A fiduciary is defined as an advisor that puts the client's interest ahead of their own. They will charge a fee based on your assets under management. Often, you will find RIAs with a firm like Charles Schwab that refer you based upon your investment objectives.

3. Robo-Advisors

Online robo-advisors are good for people with less than $100,000 to invest. It is an economical way to get financial advice and allows you to put together a portfolio that grows over time. Some of the major benefits are lower costs and ease of use. Typically, you are given a questionnaire to complete and get back a plan you can implement based on your answers. Fees can start as low as 25 basis points (a quarter of 1%) or 0.25%. So, for example, if you had a portfolio of $100,000, you would pay $250 per year.

The type of advisor best for you will often depend on how much money you have to work with. If you have a small dollar amount of $25,000, a robo-advisor would be best for you. If you have more than that, a full-service advisor or an RIA might work for you. Each firm will have different minimums, so that should be one of the first things you ask about when you are screening advisors.

How Do You Pay Your Advisor? Fee Versus Commission

When it comes to investing your money, you are going to pay a fee or a commission—there's little difference between the two. Most advisors work on a commission basis, which will include the fees they are charging as well.

Here's how it works. The financial advisor collects a percentage of the charges or fees you are paying for his or her services. Thus, if you pay a fee of $2,000 or pay commissions for $75, the financial advisor collects a percentage of that fee, which would typically be around 35% to 45% of the overall fee.

There are two ways to invest:

1. **Transaction-based**. This is where you pay a commission in

a client-directed account for each trade. "Client-directed" means that you as the client approve each trade and some of the trades could be your own ideas.

2. **Management fee.** This is a percentage fee based on the value of your account. It applies to managed accounts and includes all trading expenses as well as the fee for having your account professionally managed based on your objectives. You've probably seen the ad on TV where the investment firm proudly touts that they only make more money when you make more money. This is a perfect example of a managed account. The bottom line is it puts everyone on the same page. If the account value goes down, the management fee will be less and vice versa. As an example, if you have a $1 million account that is being managed and the fee is 1%, you will pay $10,000 per year and the financial advisor will make around $4,000 of that.

Beware the Churn

Churning is a devious way financial advisors can increase their commissions by placing several buy and sell orders within the same account—often in the same day—which only benefits the advisor making more commissions. Reverse churning is just the opposite, meaning you have a managed account and there are no trades taking place. It tends to defeat the point. If you are paying a management fee and no trades take place month after month, what are you paying for? This is akin to paying for nothing. All you are really doing is making your advisor rich.

I remember meeting with a prospective client who had an RIA as an advisor. She had purchased a mutual fund over a year earlier and the RIA was charging her a monthly management fee. I thought, what exactly was the point of charging a fee to "manage" the fund on top of the management fee the mutual fund was already charging? It was a particularly well-performing fund and, as time went forward, if the advisor told her to sell the fund to buy another, she would be stuck paying a monster capital gains tax. In addition, the fee the RIA was charging was hurting the client's overall return.

Commissions

Two investment products stand out as having the highest commissions paid to the financial advisor: annuities and life insurance. Personally, I have never liked annuities for two reasons. The first is there are internal fees contained with the annuity. The second is there are excessive fees if you want to pull money out of the annuity early—generally within seven years of purchase. These fees are known as a contingent deferred sales charge (CDSC) and can start as high as 7% of your principal and gradually go down to zero.

Most annuities allow you to take out 10% of your principal per year without penalty. Also, remember when you are finally able to withdraw all your funds from the annuity without any fees, the potential increase in value will be taxed as ordinary income.

Life insurance, on the other hand, is an extremely complicated product. I liked life insurance because it allows the client to better prepare for potential estate taxes. In the case where life insurance is warranted, I would strongly urge you to work only with a firm that has access to multiple carriers. In this way, they can shop for the best life insurance at the lowest possible premium for your needs rather than being tied exclusively to one carrier.

Open Architecture

You only want to work with an investment firm that has open architecture. This means the firm does not have a personal stake in working with one manager over another. When I worked at Merrill

Lynch, we had no internal managers. All our managers were from outside our firm. They were highly vetted and monitored, and there was no vested interest in working with one over another. In fact, if they did not perform well and obtain sound investment results, or if they deviated from the agreed investment style, we would terminate their contract and move those assets to a different manager.

I'm not so sure all investment firms are the same—in fact I know of one that uses only internal investment managers. The problem with this is if they don't perform well, they will not fire themselves, thus you are at their mercy. I was told my firm actually interviewed Bernie Madoff because his results were "so good." We did not hire him as a manager, thank goodness, because he could not provide an appropriate audit of his results. We always performed a thorough audit of any new investment firms we were considering adding to our platform. Bernie did not pass muster.

A few years ago, one of my most astute clients raised the issue of possible financial fraud with managed accounts. He wanted to understand how he would know if outside managers were illegally withdrawing funds from his investment account. Would we monitor that kind of activity? This was an easy question to answer, and I want to reiterate it for you because it's an important factor in choosing an investment advisor. What I explained to my client is that at Merrill and virtually all other large investment firms, there is a firewall between the firm you are working with and the outside managers.

So, when you are protected by a large institution, outside managers do not have access to any of your funds. All they can do is instruct the firm to place buys and sells in your account based on your investment objectives. All the monies and trades stay within the firm you are working with. Thus, there can be no fraud when it comes to your managed investment account.

This is in direct contrast to some of the smaller boutique firms

I competed with over the years where there was no firewall. Their managers were able to place trades based on the client's objectives, but it was done in-house and there was no oversight from a larger firm that protects the assets from unwanted interference. Not only does that increase the risk of fraud, but there is no oversight on performance either. If your returns are poor, a smaller house is not going to fire itself.

I remember competing with a small firm that had only one person as their investment manager. I thought, how in the heck can a single person put together stock portfolios and try to achieve promising results? The answer? They can't. There are only so many hours in a work week to research and obtain the best possible results for the client. Larger management firms will have teams of research analysts who guide the portfolio managers in the decision-making process. One-man bands are dangerous when it comes to your money.

Do Your Due Diligence!

If you are working with an investment advisor at a major firm, it's easy to check the investment advisor's background. Go to the Financial Industry Regulatory Authority (FINRA) website (https://brokercheck.finra.org/). Then enter your investment advisor's name. It will tell you if there are any complaints or problems with that advisor. If you find there are numerous complaints and settlements—meaning a cash payout to settle a complaint—connected with an advisor, I would not do business with that person.

Be forewarned that there are different requirements and disclosure regulations for traditional stockbrokers who are now often referred to as advisors or RIAs in the brokerage world. RIAs do not have to disclose customer complaints, civil lawsuits, or arbitrations, thus making it hard to discern if the RIA has had past dealings that were not favorable for their clientele.

How Do I Go About Locating a Good Financial Advisor?

The most obvious way to find a financial advisor is to ask for a referral from someone you know and respect. As I see it, referrals can come from one of three sources. First, you could ask friends, but make sure you ask your most affluent friend, one who is knowledgeable about the investment world. Don't just ask for a name—ask about the advisor's service, the returns, periodic reviews, and follow-through.

Another source of referrals could come from your CPA. They most likely know and have established a relationship with an advisor they would be happy to refer you to. Lastly, you may ask to speak to a branch manager at one of the major investment firms located in your area. The manager will be more than happy to assist and can refer you to a financial advisor within their firm.

Be sure to have investment goals in mind when you speak to your CPA or your local branch manager. Do you want a fixed-income portfolio? A growth portfolio tilted toward stocks? Retirement planning? Or something else? Be sure to ask for a specialist in the kind of investment you are most interested in.

There are several investment websites available that offer services that can match you with a financial advisor in your area, but be careful. I went to one of these websites, gave them my information, and they matched me with three advisors in my area. The problem I had with this was they were all at very small boutique firms and, personally, I would have no comfort level whatsoever with the small firms. They may all be fine and ethical people but, remember, fraud generally occurs in small firms, not in large ones.

You may not have a perfect investment result when dealing with a large firm, but the odds of having fraud on your accounts are diminished and—God forbid—if there *was* fraud in your account, it would be rectified posthaste. The large firms are genuinely concerned about their reputation and will watch out to make sure you are treated fairly and honestly.

What Do You Do When You're Not Satisfied with Your Current Financial Advisor?

Leaving an advisor is not as complicated as it may sound. What you need to do is simply review the steps we talked about when choosing a financial advisor and then transfer your account to that new financial advisor. The transfer of the account is simple. You give your new financial advisor a copy of your most recent statement from your existing account and he or she will provide you with the transfer form which you will sign. This is known as an ACAT or account-transfer form.

What happens then is your new financial advisor's back office will send that transfer form to your existing financial advisor, and they will be obligated to transfer your assets to the new firm of your choice. Assuming all goes well, this will typically take less than two weeks. And, if you are so inclined, you do not have to contact your previous financial advisor—no phone calls are required to transfer your account.

Listed below are 12 suggestions I strongly recommend following when you are looking for an investment advisor. Remember, this is not a marriage—if you are uncomfortable for any reason with your chosen advisor, you can always look for another one and follow the procedures outlined above.

Golden Strategies

1. Make sure you are aware of all fees regarding your investments.

2. Make sure you are fully aware of your advisor's background and the firm he or she works for.
3. Is your advisor really listening to you and do they care? I tried to treat every client as if they were my best friend's widow. Think about that!
4. Make sure you get a written proposal and share it with someone you trust.
5. Ask if you can bring a confidant to the next meeting. If not, run for the door!
6. Be willing to provide your most recent statement, but be aware that any financial advisor can poke holes in how you've invested your money in the past.
7. Inquire about sales goals. In other words, are there rewards for the financial advisor if they offer a certain investment?
8. Get a review of your account from your financial advisor at least every six months—preferably, every three months.
9. Call your advisor back when they call you. It might be important. I remember all too often when clients did not bother to return important calls.
10. Work with a team of advisors and make sure at least two of them have 10 or more years' experience. This way, you will receive better input and, of course, those advisors will have seen it all.
11. Avoid working with a bank financial advisor. This will typically be the lone advisor working in a bank branch. The reason for this is because they are often new to the industry and will not have enough experience to advise you properly.
12. Inquire whether the advisor has any professional credentials such as a CPA (Certified Public Accountant), CFP (Certified Financial Planner), or CFA (Charter Financial Analyst). These designations are difficult to obtain and speak volumes about the advisor's background. The advisor may also have

some designations they obtained from the firm they work for, which would also be a plus.

Workshop Topics

1. Go to the FINRA website and, under BrokerCheck, type in a random name and scan the history of that advisor. Have they changed firms many times? Have there been complaints against them? Was a financial settlement involved? How many states are they licensed in? This information will prove invaluable in determining whether you want to entrust your hard-earned money to that person.
2. Call a local firm, ask to speak to the manager, and set up an appointment. During the appointment, inquire why you should do business with that firm and what they offer that other firms do not. Have the manager recommend an advisor to set up a second appointment. Do this more than once—you will be surprised how much you learn and how much you already knew in the first place!

GOLDEN RULE 5

BUILD A BUFFER

Preparing for the Inevitable

The unexpected is an inevitable part of life. Let's face it kids, shit happens. And yes, reality can happen to you, just as it happened to Harold Lloyd, and just as it does and will happen to everyone at some point. So, when the worst happens, or the bills come due, or the wolf is at the door, you need access to funds—often in a hurry. Building your buffer requires savings and assets, of course, but it also requires agility and an ability to shift along with the winds of change.

Let me tell you about a person who illustrates the need for a buffer very well. While many may not remember his name now, Harold Lloyd was one of the biggest stars of the silent movie era, largely—and ironically—because of his ability to speak to the cultural moment and pivot along with the trends and technology of the day.

Lloyd made over 200 films, including dozens of successful comedy shorts as an ultra-rich and ambitious go-getter named Lonesome Luke in big goofy glasses who was always chasing the brass ring but forever getting in his own way.[47] The lovable loser, much like Charlie Chaplin's Tramp, matched perfectly with the mood of the moment in the Roaring Twenties and was wildly successful.

Lloyd was also a daredevil, famous for performing his own stunts. Unfortunately, during filming at the height of his career, a real bomb was accidentally used as a prop and blew up, badly disfiguring Lloyd's face and severing the thumb and index finger on his right hand. But did that stop the resourceful and agile Harold Lloyd? No, it did not. He turned his adversity into opportunity and created a whole new character called Harold Glass.

Of course, the studio was furious. Lonesome Luke was a proven box office hit, a real moneymaker—and when Harold Lloyd told them he wanted to swap out a sure bet like Luke for an untested character, they objected loudly. But Lloyd was an innovator. He understood the cultural tide was turning away from wealthy characters and toward screen idols that audiences could relate to in their everyday lives.

Harold Glass was a deeper character, more human, with greater emotional depth and genuine feelings. This was a leap forward in motion pictures—heroes that were more accessible to Great Depression-era audiences. Lloyd pioneered the idea of the more human everyman on the screen, someone just like the people in the audience, rather than the two-dimensional characters who were removed from reality and projected from a world far above the audience's experience.

When his studio objected, Lloyd took his show on the road and started his own studio, merging with Pathé Pictures, which later merged with Paramount. He turned out to be right on the money, and Harold Glass became a bigger star than Lonesome Luke had

[47] Annette D'Agostino Lloyd, "Fires and Pathé and Greenacres—with Many Casualties," *Harold Lloyd Dot US*, accessed September 28, 2024, https://haroldlloyd.us/the-films/the-state-of-the-lloyd-films/.

ever been. Glass was so successful that Luke was eventually phased out. Part of Lloyd's secret sauce was he offered his films in a new format—less expensive single reel shorts. He was not only creatively agile but technologically as well, delivering stories to audiences in a new and more accessible way.

As a result, Harold Lloyd became one of the wealthiest men in Hollywood during one of the most difficult economic downturns in this country and he lived like the Wolf of Hollywood Boulevard. He married a hot leading lady named Mildred Davis, had three beautiful—and I do mean really beautiful—children, and built a palace, Green Acres, in the Hollywood Hills. It was the Pacific Coast version of the Great Gatsby's cathedral to decadence, with 44 rooms, 26 bathrooms, 12 gardens, a golf course, and a state-of-the-art film archive.

The gardens at Green Acres were famous, and the little children's cottage he built for his daughter—who once played there with Shirley Temple—was straight out of a Beatrix Potter story, complete with a miniature pony. And, of course, there was a ballroom where all the glittering stars of the day could gather, crowned by a perpetually decorated and brightly illuminated Christmas tree. I dined at Green Acres once, beneath that tree. It felt like I had stepped back in time. Harold Lloyd's mansion is now an event space run by the town, which should give you a hint about what happened to Harold Lloyd's impressive fortune.

Time marches on, of course, and so does technology—and the economy. Harold Lloyd's lucrative silent classics became anachronisms. His iconic character Harold Glass was inextricably bound to a time and place that was no more. Harold Glass became the only thing you can never afford to become in Hollywood—irrelevant.

All the business agility that had put Harold Lloyd at the top of a difficult game for decades deserted him. He turned down offer after offer because he refused to have his films displayed in theatres that could not provide pipe-organ accompaniment, which was how silent reels played best. But, of course, pipe organs were becoming obsolete in a new generation of theatres built for talking pictures that didn't need an organ playing in the background.

That was the end of one of the most meteoric careers of a generation. From that point forward, Harold Lloyd dedicated himself to the meticulous preservation of his art form, although by that point nobody but Harold cared very much.

Efforts at a revival in the 1940s failed, and Harold Lloyd retired into the luxurious passageways of his estate and closed the door. His income dwindled. Miraculously, there was a renewed interest in his films in the 1960s, but the profits never came close to what he needed to maintain his magnificent estate. He only managed to hold on to Green Acres by begging the City Council to reduce his property taxes. The land was ultimately subdivided, leaving only the house itself, the formal gardens, and the little child's cottage. There was also a revocable trust with an endowment that was just enough to preserve the quality and integrity of his films.[48]

I tell you this story about Harold Lloyd because the estate of Harold Lloyd was administered by the trust department of the United California Bank (UCB) where I worked as an accountant. It was my very first job out of college. I met Lloyd's descendants, administered what little was left of a once great fortune, and attended a Christmas party at his home with the new owners.

---

48 "The Biography of Harold Clayton Lloyd," *Harold Lloyd Dot US*, accessed September 28, 2024, https://haroldlloyd.us/the-life/the-biography-of-harold-clayton-lloyd/; "Greenacres – Harold Lloyd Estate," The Legendary Estates of Beverly Hills, accessed September 28, 2024, https://thelegendaryestatesofbeverlyhills.com/blogs/excerpts/39504389-greenacres-harold-lloyd-estate; *New World Encyclopedia*, "Harold Lloyd," last modified June 25, 2024, https://www.newworldencyclopedia.org/entry/Harold_Lloyd.

The rise and reticence of Harold Lloyd is a great lesson about what can happen when you fail to consider your liquidity needs and your time horizon. Harold Lloyd lost his fortune and nearly lost the roof over his head because he did not adjust his investments to his liquidity needs, and he failed to take the passage of time into account. These mistakes are fatal to wealth creation and preservation.

I always asked my clients right up front what their liquidity needs were, and we took those needs into account with every investment we make. Different types of business models or lifestyles require distinct levels of liquidity. Some people in this town might not work for months until the next movie comes along. They need more ready cash on hand than those with regular pay checks and a corporate job.

When it comes to investments, just as in life, time and liquidity are unavoidable. Unavoidable and immutable facts will govern the physics of your wealth.

What Is Your Time Horizon?

In 1964, the Rolling Stones released a song called "Time Is on My Side." A decade later, in 1976, the Steve Miller Band released a song entitled "Fly Like an Eagle (Time Keeps on Slipping into the Future)." About now you're asking yourself, why am I bringing up two rock 'n' roll songs devoted to time? Because when it comes to investing your money, time can be your ally or your worst enemy.

Consider my friend Mike. He is an independent auto dealer and deals exclusively in classic cars. Several years ago, his advisor told him to invest in the stock market. Unfortunately, his advisor was trying to be a hero and had not considered Mike's time horizon. Ultimately, Mike needed those funds to buy more cars and was forced to sell his stocks at an unbelievably bad time in the market. Investing is for the long run and certainly not for people who need ready access to their funds to keep their businesses afloat. Investing in the stock market *requires* a long-term horizon of at least five years. The number one rule in managing risk is to have time on your side.

There is an old saying that time is money, and that's true in ways you might not have thought about before. Time is the backdrop against which your money grows. It is time that will determine the investment decisions you make, where to place your funds, and which house to buy. When you are younger, you can take more risk and, conversely, in retirement years you will want to take less risk. How are you going to manage your money so you can live comfortably today and even more comfortably tomorrow?

In a recent *USA Today* article, it was noted that half of American families have *no* money set aside for retirement.[49] In other words, they live off Social Security and potentially a pension from their former employer. Only 14% of Americans have saved over $100,000[50] and only one family in 1,000 has saved over $5,000,000 for retirement.[51] These numbers are a little frightening! The bottom line is most people fail to plan, thus leading to no plan and guaranteed failure. But that isn't going to happen to you because you are reading this book.

---

[49] Jessica Guynn, "The Retirement Savings Crisis: Why More Americans Can't Afford to Stop Working," *USA Today*, July 10, 2024, https://www.usatoday.com/story/money/2024/07/10/why-americans-cannot-afford-retirement/74303336007/.

[50] Jacob Wade, "How Many Americans Have $100,000 for Retirement?," Yahoo! Finance, last modified April 13, 2023, https://finance.yahoo.com/news/many-americans-100-000-saved-192658338.html.

[51] Veronica Dagher, "Here's What a $5 Million Retirement Looks Like in America," *Wall Street Journal*, August 11, 2023, https://www.wsj.com/articles/heres-what-a-5-million-retirement-looks-like-in-america-1abc76d9.

Frank's Success Savings Plan

The first thing I suggest is to establish a rainy-day fund. This is your emergency money and should be easily accessible and not subject to any type of market risk. By market risk I mean having to sell the asset at the current market value, which may be more or less than you started with. These funds should only be placed in a money market account that can be accessed easily by writing a check.

When I retired at the end of 2021, money markets were paying 0.1%. Today, they are a little over 5%.[52] So, while your rainy-day money sits there, it at least earns a reasonable amount of interest in today's marketplace. There has been a lot of discussion about how much you should have in your rainy-day money market account, but six months' worth of income would certainly be a reasonable starting point.

Next, I would urge you to consider having an automatic deduction from your paycheck that would go directly into a 401(k) or an IRA or even a simple money market account that can be accessed to invest those funds for retirement. If the funds are deducted before you see the money, it's much easier to build savings. Out of sight, out of mind.

What about credit? As someone who spent most of my career working for a bank, I was incredibly careful about using credit to finance any purchase. I felt strongly that it would be horribly bad if I had difficulties repaying the money I owed to my employer and never wanted to take that risk. I financed two homes and several cars through my employer. I'm grateful I never missed a payment and everything worked out very well for both parties.

When it comes to credit, I suggest borrowing money only to

52 "US Money Market Treasury Yield (I:USMMAR)," YCharts, accessed September 28, 2024, https://ycharts.com/indicators/us_money_market_account_rate.

purchase a home, buy a car, or start a business. That means keeping your credit card balance well below the allowable amount. And when it comes to buying something, do not just look at the monthly payment, look at what the overall cost is. Use credit wisely and do like your parents probably told you when you got your first credit card—only use it in case of emergency. Always ask yourself at least a dozen times before you sign the dotted line—can I repay this loan?

Above all, preserve your savings and let some time go by. The amount of time you can let your money sit and grow without spending it is called your time horizon. It really works to your benefit, which is why it's so beneficial to start saving when you're young. Your time horizon will often dictate which types of investments are appropriate for you based on how long you can let the money sit before you need to access those funds.

If you know you have big payments coming due at certain times of the year, prepare for that eventuality. I had several clients who wanted to have a fund set aside for paying their taxes by April 15th each year. In every case, I suggested they purchase a U.S. Treasury Bill that matured slightly before April 15th. In that case, the client needed to be extremely conservative to make sure their funds were readily available when they were due. In no way should the client invest in anything that had a potential for fluctuation in market value.

If you have saved enough to be able to put money aside for a longer timeframe, you might want to invest in long-term bonds or the stock market. An appropriate time to invest in the stock market would be when you have money in your 401(k) and you are 30 years old. Another example would be opening a 529 plan for a newborn grandchild. Here you should certainly invest in the stock market as well, given that you will have a long time frame of 18 years. In this case, I would suggest an age-based portfolio. This is where the ratio between stocks and bonds narrows as the child ages and has all the funds in bonds when they turn 18 and enroll in college.

The Nuts and Bolts of Bonds

Bonds are different than other types of investments in one major way. Instead of buying shares in a company, you are essentially lending money to a company or, in some cases, a municipality or our own federal government. Right away, this obviously implies less risk. You're not throwing your lot in with the fortunes of a company, rather, you're lending money for a fixed period of time with a guarantee that you will get paid back—with interest. You are the loaner, not the loanee, and that puts you in a different position with respect to your investment.

Bonds are still considered an investment because there is some risk involved. The company could go bankrupt and the value of the bond will fluctuate until it matures, but outside of unforeseen and catastrophic circumstances, you are most likely to get your investment back at maturity. Described below are two of my favorite clients who invested in municipal bonds. Most of my clients were more interested in low-risk investments like bonds rather than stocks. They made their fortunes elsewhere, not by investing. Given the clients' high tax bracket, municipal bonds were a perfect investment for both.

Profiles in Prosperity

Loyd Sigmon. I was introduced to Loyd Sigmon by the trust department of Security Pacific Bank. Sigmon had enjoyed an amazing career. He was General Dwight Eisenhower's chief communications officer during World War II, and later served as executive vice president with Gene Autry's Golden West broadcasters which owned eight radio and two television stations on the West Coast, including KMPC 710.

Loyd coined the phrase SIGALERT: a warning that is broadcast to this very day throughout Southern California to alert drivers of gridlock on the freeway system. Ironically, he told me more than once that although he was best remembered for the SIGALERT, he felt that was one of his minor accomplishments. I had lunch with him many times at his home in Sherman Oaks where Carmen, his housekeeper, would prepare us lunch and he would share his philosophies on life and business with me. He used to say, "It is important to do business in person so you can look them in the eye"—a philosophy that had served him very well. He understood that human contact was an integral part of good business and a good life.

Aubra Tilley was the founder of Input/Output, a leading provider of seismic imaging technology used by oil and gas companies for the exploration and development of offshore and onshore reservoirs. They offered imaging solutions ranging from design and planning seismic surveys to the acquisition and processing of seismic data.

Aubra & Dorothy Tilley

A note that I received from Aubra on 2/12/2015: Frank, Your impact has been far greater than I can express. Thanks so much.

I met Tilley while I was working at Security Pacific Bank. He was a true gentleman and one I enjoyed very much. I'll never forget how he would always answer the phone: "Tilley here." One of the things I remember most about our work together was when he purchased a $100,000 annuity for his housekeeper, providing her with around $600 a month for the rest of her life, which was a great help to her. This was one time where I felt the purchase of an annuity made perfect sense.

Both of these remarkable individuals, who I was lucky enough to call clients, were interested in preserving their money rather than growing their wealth, so they invested heavily in bonds. They also used their businesses and their wealth to make the world a better place. This brings home the concept of determining what your primary goal is. Do you want to grow your money by investing in stocks? Or do you want to preserve your money by investing in bonds?

Here are some of the fundamental facts about bonds.

Maturity Date

When you purchase a bond, there will be a maturity date or a fixed point in time when the face value of your principal proceeds is paid back to you. Basically, what happens then is the obligation is satisfied, your agreement with the company is terminated, you are paid back, and you will earn no future interest.

Coupon

The coupon determines the rate at which you will be earning money. Most bonds pay interest semiannually. Your payment dates will be on the maturity date and six months before or after that date. If your maturity date is September 1, 2030, your payment dates will be March 1st and September 1st.

Tax Status

Taxability varies depending upon which type of bond you purchase. If you buy a U.S. Treasury Bond, interest will be state tax free but you will still owe the Feds. If you buy a corporate bond, interest will be fully taxable. Certain federal agencies like Federal Home Loan Bank and Federal Farm Credit and Tennessee Valley Authority are state tax free, whereas the rest are fully taxable. Municipal bonds are federally tax free but may be state taxable.

Callability

Most bonds have a call date. What this means is the entity can call your bonds away from you and you will be paid the principal proceeds on the call date. There are generally two reasons bonds are called. First is the issuing entity can refinance at a much lower rate of interest. Secondly, the issuing entity has the ability financially to retire the debt. Unfortunately, you have no say so whatsoever when it comes to your bond being called. And because of the refinancing at lower rates when your bond is called away, you generally cannot replace your bond with the same rate of interest you were originally earning.

There are several types of bonds and it's important to know a little something about each. So here are the basics.

1. Treasuries

I love U.S. Treasuries because there's very little risk in purchasing government bonds. The only real risk is if you sell the bond prior to maturity, you may not get back all your principal as they are subject to an interest-rate risk. While the government guarantees interest along the way and full value at maturity, it does not guarantee the market value of treasuries if you've sold prior to maturity. Remember, with bonds of any type, the longer the maturity, the more they will fluctuate in value given changes in interest rates.

Treasuries Come in Four Flavors

- **Treasury Bills**. Treasury Bills have maturities less than one year and are sold at a discount. This means if you buy a $10,000 Treasury Bill and you paid $9,800 for it, upon maturity you will be paid $10,000 of which $200 is the interest you earned from the bill.
- **Treasury Notes**. Treasury Notes have maturities that range from one to 10 years and interest is paid semiannually. They are offered at face value, which means if you pay 100%, or par, you are guaranteed to get back what you invested.
- **Treasury Bonds**. Treasury Bonds have maturities that range from 10 to 30 years and interest is paid twice a year.
- **TIPS**. TIPS, also known as Treasury Protected Inflation Securities, are issued with maturity dates of five, 10, and 30 years and, again, interest is paid twice a year. You could also invest in different maturities in the secondary market, which is the market for bonds that have been resold after they were originally issued. That would apply to all types of treasuries as well.

  TIPS offer an inflation hedge. While they do have a fixed rate of interest, your principal value increases or decreases daily based on changes in the Consumer Price Index (CPI). An example would be if you purchased $10,000 of TIPS with a maturity of five years and the CPI was up 2% each year. At maturity, your principal value would be worth a little more than $11,000 because of compounding. In doing the math, the interest amount is calculated by multiplying the interest by the current principal value based on the CPI increase.

As an example, let's say you purchased 10 TIPS or $10,000 worth, the inflation rate was 2%, and you are now into the second year. The interest amount would be calculated by taking 102% times 2% and this would earn you $102 for your first semi annual payment. It would then adjust your second payment for the year based upon the current CPI principal value amount. If you are in your third year and the inflation rate was 3%, your interest amount would be calculated as follows: 105 x 2% which would earn you $210 yearly or $105 every 6 months.

Remember that all U.S. Treasuries are state tax free. Another benefit to treasuries is that, at maturity, you are guaranteed to get back the entire face amount. There is no FDIC limit of $250,000 on your principal amount because U.S. Treasuries are guaranteed for the full amount of face value at maturity.

2. Municipal Bonds

Municipal bonds are instruments issued by municipalities, which include states, utilities, cities, water districts, school districts, highways, etc. The interest from municipal bonds is exempt from federal taxes. If the bond was purchased from the state you reside in, interest will be state tax free as well. If you reside in a state like Florida that has no state income taxes, interest will be both federal and state income tax free. Another advantage of living in a state with no income taxes is you can purchase bonds from any state, thus giving you many more choices. Be forewarned, however, if you live in California and buy a bond from any other state, your interest will be state taxable. This is true for any state in the union that has a state income tax.

Taxable Equivalent Yield (TEY)

TEY is the return a taxable bond needs for its yield to equal the yield on a tax-exempt bond like a municipal. Or, to put it another way, what are your net earnings after paying taxes on the taxable bond? How much of your money do you get to keep? This is important to know as it is a key factor in determining which type of bond you want to invest in.

Thus, if you have an income of $1,000,000, you live in California, and you earn 5% on an in-state municipal bond, your taxable equivalent would be 10.06%. That means if you earned 10.06%, you would net 5% after paying taxes. You can check your own situation by using the website https://www.morganstanley.com/wealth-investmentsolutions/municipalbonds. Remember to use your taxable income tax bracket after your deductions for calculation purposes.

When I got into the investment business in 1982, I specialized in municipal bonds. Back then, a client could purchase a bond paying up to 11% in California. The taxable equivalency was around 22%. What that meant was after you paid taxes on a taxable investment you netted 11%. Sadly, when I retired, interest on high-quality long term municipals had gone down to around 2.75%.

3. Federal Agencies

Federal Agency bonds are from institutions like Federal Home Loan Bank, Federal Farm Credit, Tennessee Valley Authority, Federal Home Loan Mortgage Corporation, and Federal National Mortgage Association. While these bonds do not have a government guarantee, there is an implicit guarantee, meaning if these bonds were to default, that could affect the credit worthiness of treasuries in investors' eyes as well.

4. Corporate Bonds

Corporate bonds are issued by corporations and will involve the most risk, particularly relating to their credit worthiness. You should only buy corporate bonds from well-established major corporations that have a long history of minimizing credit risk. However, some corporate bonds fall into the high-yield category.

I do *not* recommend purchasing these types of bonds on your own.

In 2008 and 2009 I experienced credit risk firsthand—more than at any other time in my career. I remember clients who had GMAC bonds—the financial arm of General Motors at the time—issued to help finance car purchases. There was extreme concern that they would not pay principal when the bonds matured. Some of my clients had major positions in GMAC, and they ultimately did pay off, but it was very worrisome to say the least. As a result, I do not recommend high-yield corporate bonds which are often referred to as junk bonds for very good reason. Too often, they are total garbage that serve the seller rather than the buyer.

Bond Credit Ratings

Most bonds have a credit rating. Bonds of a stronger credit quality will be rated A or better. I would never suggest investing in a bond that is non-rated.

There are three major agencies that rate the credit worthiness of bonds. They are Moody's, Standard & Poor's, and Fitch. Listed here is the credit rating scale for bonds from Standard & Poor's.

Letter Grade	Capacity to repay
AAA	Extremely strong
AA+, AA, AA-	Very strong
A+, A, A-	Strong
BBB+, BBB, BBB-	Adequate
BB+, BB	Faces major future uncertainties
B	Faces major uncertainties
CCC	Currently vulnerable
CC	Currently highly vulnerable
C	Has filed bankruptcy protection
D	In default

Another way to look at credit ratings is to ask which bonds are investment grade. What investment grade means is you can borrow against the bonds should you need to raise money for any reason. These are the bonds rated BBB- or better. Borrowing entails using your investment account and borrowing against the securities in your account.

I've always felt if you're able to borrow against your bonds, it will give you some comfort level from the perspective of a decent credit level. This is because either a bank or an investment allows you to borrow against them. They would not allow you to borrow against them if they felt the bonds being used as collateral were in potential jeopardy. It also means you are likely to have bonds that will pay your principal balance at maturity. Just to be on the safe side when it comes to investing in bonds, I recommend only bonds rated A or better.

It's important to remember that credit ratings can change over time. Just because a bond is rated AAA today, there is no guarantee it will be rated AAA tomorrow, so keep an eye on the ratings to make sure you're up to date. On my clients' monthly statements, we listed the credit rating on every bond in their portfolio. That made it easier to monitor the credit worthiness of their bonds. We also included the approximate market value of the bonds. I would suggest keeping an eye on current values as well.

Several municipal bonds offer credit insurance. What this means is if they default, the municipal bond insurance will make you whole. The caveat is that during the Great Recession of 2008 and 2009, many of the insurers had great difficulties paying claims, and some even declared bankruptcy. So, be forewarned—make sure you know the underlying credit rating of the bonds you are considering investing in. It is safer and better never to need insurance to cover the credit of your bonds in the first place.

The Numbers and Definitions Behind Bonds

The face value of a bond is the amount of money you will receive at maturity. This will be printed on your confirmation of purchase or sale and as a line item on the activity portion of your statement. Also included will be the price you paid for the bond, the maturity date, and the yield to maturity or the call date. After the bond is purchased, the value will fluctuate to a higher or lower price—or sometimes both—and that will be measured by the price that is the percentage value of the bond. For a bond that was for $100,000, for example, if interest rates on newly issued bonds moved lower, the value would move above 100% and vice versa.

Price

The price of a bond is defined as a percentage of face value. When you invest in bonds, you will pay one of three prices. You'll either buy bonds at par or 100%, at a price below 100% that would be considered a discount, or at a price above 100% that would be considered a premium. If you buy bonds at 100%, you will receive the full face value back at maturity, assuming the entity does in fact pay you back.

Yield or Yield to Maturity

Yield to maturity is a calculation that shows you what you will be earning if you hold your bond to maturity. It considers the appreciation or depreciation of the bond at maturity plus the interest you earned on the bond. Thus, if you buy bonds at a discount, your yield to maturity will be greater than the coupon rate and visa-versa—if you buy bonds at a premium, your yield will be less than the coupon rate. Finally, if you pay par, your yield will be the same as the coupon.

Interest

Your interest rate, also known as the coupon, is most often a fixed rate. The interest rate you earn on your bonds will be clearly marked on the confirmation of purchase and on your statements. There are many exceptions to this, and they are typically identified as floating-rate interest bonds. Interest is paid on a semiannual basis and the calculation is simple: If you have invested in a $100,000 bond and the interest rate is 4%, you will receive $2,000 every six months.

Duration

This is a fancy term that can seem a bit complicated, but it's just a way of measuring how much fluctuation the bond will experience in value given any changes in interest rates. To give you an example, say interest rates move up by 1%. The value would go down by around 5% for a bond with five years left to go before it matures.

Another way to look at this is by the percentage of value the bond will increase or decrease based on interest rates changing by 1%. Thus, if you have a long-term bond and interest rates move up, the value will go down accordingly. The duration will be the amount that the price changes, given the change in interest rates. This will also be used to calculate the bond price change when interest rates move lower.

Risks Inherent in Bonds

While bonds are a much lower-risk investment than stocks, there is some risk involved. For example, if interest rates move higher, the value of your bonds will depreciate. Conversely, if interest rates move lower, the value of your bonds will appreciate. Keep in mind that the longer the maturity of the bond, the more fluctuation you will see both upward and downward. It's like a teeter totter—as one end goes up the other end goes down, an inverse ratio. More importantly, the longer the arm of the teeter totter—meaning a longer maturity—the greater the percentage of change up or down.

Thankfully, I have not experienced many times during my career when interest rates moved higher, which always leads to depreciation in the value of bonds. However, in 2022, while I was writing this book, interest rates rose significantly and I saw a corresponding loss in the value of my own bonds. So, if you feel rates moving higher, you may want to postpone your purchase of bonds. The best time to purchase bonds is when interest rates are high. And if interest rates move lower after your purchases, the value of your bonds will appreciate, thus giving you an additional benefit. The silver lining is even if the values of your bonds depreciate, they will mature at full face value, which is par or 100%.

Credit/Default Risk

There is a potential risk of not being paid back your principal at maturity. This happens most commonly with corporate bonds. This is accompanied by a lowering of the credit quality of that particular entity. If the credit quality is lowered by one of the major rating agencies, that typically will affect the bond value in a negative way.

If you are buying bonds on your own and see the credit quality is beginning to deteriorate and you have several years left on the bond until it matures, I would suggest selling that bond prior to maturity.

In addition, sadly, some corporate bonds default. This means they no longer pay interest and the value will plummet. This is especially true of lower credit quality bonds, which I have advised to stay away from.

Call Risk

Call risk is also known as a prepayment risk. As I mentioned, a sizable proportion of the bonds issued are callable. This means the entity can take the bonds away from you and pay you back your principal in full or, in some cases, at a premium. Remember this—it is the entity's decision to make, not yours, and it always comes at the worst possible time because you cannot invest in bonds at the same rate of interest.

If you buy bonds at a premium, you should be aware of what the yield to call is versus yield to maturity. I have seen some cases where the yield to call is less than 0.5%. When a client purchased bonds from me, we always had to disclose the worst possible yield. In other words, if the bond was purchased at a premium, we had to show the yield to the call figure on the confirmation. And we always quoted the yield to maturity as well.

Zero-Coupon Bonds

A zero-coupon bond means you do not earn interest on your bond until maturity. In other words, you won't get any semiannual interest payments—all interest is paid at maturity. Thus, if you buy a three-year zero-coupon bond with the yield of 3%, you will pay approximately $0.91 of the dollar and at maturity you will be paid back 100 cents on the dollar. Another way to look at this is if you buy

$100,000 of this bond, you will pay $91,000 today and, at maturity, you will be paid $100,000 and have earned $9,000 in interest.

Bear in mind that the major risk with buying zero-coupon bonds is they fluctuate more in market value given changes in interest rates. This may work for you or against you. Another caveat is in California, many school districts offer long-term zero-coupon bonds with maturity dates as long as 30 or 40 years. This concerned me because the school district was in effect kicking the "debt can" down the road.

They were raising money today they would not have to pay back until well into the future. Because they were not making interest payments semiannually, I had one important question: Will the school district be able to pay the investor off at maturity when the future arrives? I cannot state more strongly that an investor needs to look into the future and have a comfort level that the entity can and will pay the principal at maturity.

The chart below illustrates what happens to the value of a bond given changes in interest rates. Interest-rate-risk fluctuation is, in my estimation, the biggest risk for bond holders. I thought it would be helpful for you to see graphically what happens with the value of a bond given changes in interest rates both up and down. These numbers will hold true for any type of bond—corporate, municipal, or government. Remember that even if you buy U.S. government bonds, values will fluctuate until they mature. While the government guarantees return of principal at maturity plus interest, the government does not guarantee the market value of their securities should you need to sell them at any point prior to maturity.

Kudos to the website http://wolframalpha.com/
for their excellent bond yield calculator.

Bond Valuation Changes

3% Coupon

	Interest rates			
Maturity	-1%	-2%	+1%	+2%
5 years	104.7	109.7	95.5	91.2
10 years	109	118.9	91.8	84.4
15 years	112.9	127.7	88.8	79
20 years	116.4	136.1	86.3	74.8
25 years	119.5	144.1	84.2	71.6
30 years	122.4	151.7	82.6	69

5% Coupon

	Interest rates			
Maturity	-1%	-2%	+1%	+2%
5 years	104.4	109.2	95.7	91.6
10 years	108.1	117.1	92.5	85.7
15 years	111.1	124	90.2	81.6
20 years	113.6	129.9	88.4	78.6
25 years	115.7	135	87.1	76.5
30 years	117.13	139.3	86.1	75

A couple of salient points here are worth mentioning. All the numbers on the chart are percentages and a percentage of the face value. So, as an example, if you invested $100,000 in a 10-year bond with an interest rate of 3% and interest rates went down by 2% over the next five years, the value at that point would be approximately 109.7 or $109,700.

Conversely if you purchased a 30-year bond with a 5% coupon and interest rates rose by 3% over the next five years, the value would go down to $67,700. Another point worth mentioning is for managed bond accounts, the manager will invest in higher coupon bonds. This is because they are managing the portfolio for a total return number. If you look at the most extreme case, comparing a 3% bond with a 5% bond—both with maturities of 30 years left—and rates moved higher by 2%, the value of the 3% bond would go down to 69% and the value of the 5% bond would go down to 75%. So, you can see there is much less fluctuation with higher coupon bonds in terms of principal value, which is the portfolio manager's goal.

In dealing with retail bond buyers over the last 40 years, I found most clients preferred buying bonds closer to 100% or par. This means they will receive back their principal at maturity or on the call date. These clients were primarily buying bonds for income and not necessarily for a total return figure.

Another key point is if you were to buy a bond today with a 5% coupon at $0.66 on the dollar, you would have a capital gain to pay at maturity. (This would be for both federal and state, assuming you live in a state that has state income tax.) This would also hold true even if you purchased a municipal bond that produces tax-free interest. The capital gains tax would apply to all types of bonds.

Bond Swapping

A bond swap is selling one of your bonds and replacing it with another. There are two reasons to do this. The first is to take a tax loss against your gains. The second is to capture the profit on a bond that has appreciated in value since you purchased it.

For example, if you purchased a 5% coupon bond with a maturity of 35 years and over the next five years the interest rates went down by 3%, the value would go up to 167.4. Should you consider selling the bond and taking the profit? In my practice, I felt like swapping bonds was like putting together a jigsaw puzzle—however, in this jigsaw there are only two pieces of the puzzle, and both must be available. First, you need to have the bond selling at a nice profit. Secondly, and even more importantly, you need to have a bond to replace it with that makes sense.

The problem with a 30-year bond selling at 167.4 is it will be hard to find the second piece to the puzzle. To further explain this, if you had purchased $100,000 of bonds paying 5% at par or 100% and now the bond is selling at $167,400, you would probably be inclined to take the profit. Just remember the gain is subject to both state and federal tax. So, you would give about a third of that profit away, leaving you with around $44,000.

Now comes the hard part—finding a replacement. If interest rates on long-term bonds had gone to 2%, there is no way to make this swap work. Either you give up substantial income or pay a monster premium to purchase the new bond. If it's a municipal bond, you cannot write off the loss at maturity.

What I found over the years is that the most logical time to take a profit is when we could sell a bond, take the profit, and reinvest the proceeds in a longer-term bond with the same or higher coupon. You can certainly sell bonds at a profit, but the caveat if you are looking for income is to make sure you know what you are buying to replace the bond you are selling. Be sure it makes sense for your situation.

How about tax loss harvesting with bonds? Here you would sell a bond valued for less than you paid for it and purchase a new bond with (hopefully) a higher rate of interest and probably a longer maturity to capture the loss and use the loss against gains or income. Three rules come into play in avoiding the wash-sale rule, which states you cannot sell a security for a tax loss and buy it back before 30 days. If you do, you cannot take the loss. You need to buy a bond with two of the three following aspects: a different issuer, a different coupon, and a different maturity. These rules should be easy to follow.

Bond Offerings as of September 13, 2024

What follows next are offerings from the four basic types of bonds. These are treasuries, federal agencies, municipals, and corporate bonds. I felt it would be helpful for you to see actual offerings on a specific date so you could compare the different interest rates these four types of bonds were paying with approximately the same maturities. What you will find is as you extend your maturity, you earn a higher rate of interest. This is because bond values will fluctuate more, given changes in interest rates over a long maturity.

The first set of offerings are treasuries or sometimes known as U.S. Government Securities. The offerings for treasuries show you earn more as you extend maturity to 20 and 30 years. However, in this case, the one-year treasury yielding 3.78% is higher than the 10-year treasury at 3.49%. When this takes place, it is indicative of the fact that investors are predicting a recession and they want to lock in longer-term rates—because if a recession does occur, the Federal Reserve will most likely lower interest rates. As such, not only will you earn interest on the bond and lock in that attractive interest rate, you will also have appreciation in the bond as interest rates move lower. This leads me to discuss the important topic of yield curve.

U.S. Treasuries

Bond Description	Coupon	Maturity	Offer Price	Offer Yield/Code
TREASURY BILL	0	9/4/2025	96.43411111	3.78878164 \M
US TREASURY N/B	3.875	9/30/2029	102.7425277	3.27976334 \M
US TREASURY N/B	3.875	8/15/2034	103.1860896	3.49171014\M
US TREASURY N/B	4.125	8/15/2044	102.58605	3.93623325 \M
US TREASURY N/B	4.25	8/15/2054	106.28065	3.89260234 \M

Date of availability 9/13/24

Yield Curve

The yield curve is simply a graph that shows a span of years along the bottom horizontal axis and the percentage the bonds are paying on the left vertical axis. In an economy where you have growth, the yield curve could start at 2% and move higher for longer-term maturities. If the yield curve is just the opposite, meaning you start at a higher interest rate and move to a lower interest rate for longer-term maturities, this is known as an inverted yield curve. An inverted curve is an indication of a possible downturn in the economy.

The yield curve has been a strong and reliable indicator of a slowing economy and has proven to be a much better predictor of the future of the economy than a strong stock market. When the investment pros talk about reading the tea leaves, this is one of the major items many of them discuss. I suggest you look at the current yield curve for treasuries. This can easily be found on the website http://ustreasuryyieldcurve.com/.

The second set of offerings is federal agencies. These are also state tax free like treasuries, except for Fannie Mae which is fully taxable. These are very safe investments and have a good liquidity future, but like all bonds they have market risk. These agencies will typically pay a little more than treasuries, and you can certainly see that particularly with maturities 10 years and longer. Federal agencies would be ideal for investors who want to minimize risk and earn a little bit more than treasuries.

Federal Agency Bonds

Bond Description	Coupon	Maturity	Offer Price	Offer Yield/Code
FEDERAL HOME LOAN BANK	2.375	3/14/2025	98.9713472	4.50112847 \M
FEDERAL HOME LOAN BANK	4.25	7/14/2025	100.0009199	4.20733862 \C
FANNIE MAE	4	9/3/2027	100.364535	3.20079963 \C
FANNIE MAE	4.1	9/4/2029	100.48363	3.04699188 \C

FEDERAL FARM CREDIT BANK	2.85	9/13/2032	94.523905	3.64605056 \M

Date of availability 9/13/24

The third set of offerings are municipal bonds which offer tax-free interest from federal taxes and, if you purchase a bond from the state you reside in, interest will be totally tax free. The other benefit is there is little credit risk with municipalities if you buy investment-grade credit-rated bonds. This means BBB- or better. I would recommend buying at bonds that are rated A or better. You always want to minimize your credit risk because if you have just one bond that defaults in your portfolio, it will be catastrophic for your overall return. Here we see a more normal yield curve, meaning as you extend maturity, you earn a greater rate of interest.

Municipal Bonds

Bond Description	Coupon	Maturity	Offer Price	Offer Yield
CALIFORNIA ST GO BDS	5	3/1/2026	101.295	2.142C
CHINO CALIF PUB FING AUTH REV	5	9/1/2027	102.695	2.142C
HANFORD CALIF JT UN HIGH SCH	5	8/1/2029	102.897	1.648C
NOVATO CALIF UNI SCH DIST	3	8/1/2036	99.704	3.030M
BEVERLY HILLS CALIF UNI SCH	3.25	8/1/2042	100.126	3.231C

Date of availability 9/13/24

An interesting highlight is the 30-year municipal in this case is yielding just slightly less than the 30-year treasury. So if you are in a high tax bracket, municipals would surely make sense, and I would urge you to consider them as part of your portfolio. Just remember that municipal bonds come in two basic flavors: general obligation and revenue. General obligation bonds are voter approved, and the municipality has the right and obligation to raise taxes should they need to do so to pay you, the bond holder. A revenue bond is a bond backed by a stream of revenue. This may be a utility where people pay their water or electric bills, a toll road, and so on.

The last offerings I want to highlight are corporate bonds. As you can see from the offerings, you don't gain an awful lot by extending maturity. The one-year Capital One bonds are yielding 4.80% and the 17-year bond from Verizon is yielding 4.88%. The one thing to bear in mind with long-term corporate bonds is the longer the maturity, the more you increase credit risk. In other words, will Verizon be around 17 years from now to pay you or pay your beneficiaries? In looking at these bonds, I would be inclined not to buy any bonds longer than 10 years.

Corporate Bonds

Bond Description	Coupon	Maturity	Offer Price	Offer Yield/Code
CAPITAL ONE FINANCIAL CO	3.2	2/5/2025	99.38428	4.80674 M
MITSUBISHI UFJ FIN GRP	3.85	3/1/2026	99.80286	3.98946 M
KRAFT HEINZ FOODS CO	3	6/1/2026	98.57844	3.86579 M
ENERGY TRANSFER LP	3.9	7/15/2026	99.70303	4.06747 M
VERIZON COMMUNICATIONS	4.75	11/1/2041	98.395	4.88897 M

Date of availability 9/13/24

For my clients, corporate bonds were an ideal way to provide income in a nontaxable account like an IRA or other retirement account. Most of my clients invested in municipal bonds, given their high tax brackets and their objective to preserve principal. If you want the most conservative investment, stick with short-term treasuries. If you decide to have bonds as a part of your portfolio, it's best to have a working knowledge of the bond market. Remember, you can either have a bond portfolio managed by an outside money manager or you can work with an advisor like me who specialized in the fixed-income arena. In any event, I strongly recommend that bonds be a portion of your portfolio and that you increase this portion as you age to lower your investment risk.

Listed below are seven suggestions for investing in the bond market. They will provide a road map for you to follow for successful results in the bond arena.

Golden Strategies

1. Keep your maturities in sight. Remember that short-term bonds fluctuate substantially less than long-term bonds, given changes in interest rates. In my experience, most of my clients wanted longer-term bonds so they could maximize their income and ultimately give the bonds to their children.
2. Only buy high-quality bonds. Most bonds are rated by Moody's or Standard & Poor's or both. I suggest you invest in bonds rated A or better. Another way to look at this is to never buy junk. An advisor told me way back that if you live in junk you die in junk. Remember you are lending money to that entity and you obviously want to be paid back at maturity!
3. Be aware of call features. The issuing entity can call the bond away from you at the most inopportune time—when interest rates have gone lower—and they can refinance at lower rates. Remember, they pick the time, you do not.
4. Consider a bond ladder—by this I mean having bonds mature over the next 25 years or so. Have maturities in the short term so if interest rates rise, you can renew at higher rates as they mature. If interest rates move lower, you have locked in the rates with your longer-term bonds.
5. You may also consider a barbell strategy. This is when you have short-term and long-term bonds with an emphasis on longer-term bonds to maximize income. This also provides for better price performance if interest rates fall, but be forewarned that if interest rates rise, this strategy will work against you.
6. When investing in corporate bonds, find out what Wall

Street is saying about the stock of that corporation. I always did this for my clients—if we had a sell recommendation on their stock, I never recommended investing in bonds from that company.

7. Bear in mind there are only two ways to make money with bonds: interest and potential appreciation. The best way to achieve potential appreciation is to buy high-yielding bonds that have been beaten down because the corporation is doing poorly and potentially may make a comeback. I am *not* in favor of this concept due to potential default risk, which means you no longer earn interest, and your principle is *very* much at risk! It could go to *zero!*

Workshop Topics

1. Take out a piece of paper, write down $10,000, a 4% rate of interest, a maturity date of July 1, 2040, and a call date of July 1, 2030. Ask yourself how much interest you'll earn yearly. When will you get paid? How much will you get back at maturity? How much will you receive if the bond is called? What will the value be in, say, 2028? What is your overall return?
   a. Answers: $400 paid yearly and $200 paid on January 1 and July 1. You are paid $10,000 at maturity and at least $10,000 if the bond is called. Some bonds have a premium call price that could net you between $100 and $300 above the $10,000, but that provision is rare. Bond values will fluctuate over time based on two principles: interest movements and changes in credit quality. Thus, the bond may appreciate or depreciate. It might be worth $9,500 or $10,500 if sold prior to maturity, based on those two factors. Your overall return will be based on

what you paid for the bond in the first place. If you paid less than $10,000, your return would be greater than 4%. If you paid more than $10,000, your return would be less than 4%.

2. When investing in bonds, only invest in high-quality entities. That means affluent municipalities or corporations. That might sound a bit elitist, but it is your hard-earned money and this is all business. Non-negotiable!
3. Get familiar with the fluctuation in value of bonds, even on U.S. government bonds. While there is no credit risk on government bonds—also known as U.S. Treasuries—there is market risk on your bonds if sold prior to maturity. This will be based on interest-rate fluctuations.

GOLDEN RULE 6

KEEP YOUR MONEY PROTECTED!

Recognizing and Avoiding Fraud

Unfortunately, any investment book must contain a chapter on fraud so you don't wind up on the short end of the many deceptive tricks that lie in wait out there on the Internet and elsewhere. Investment fraud and money fraud have proliferated to such a degree these days that the subject demands a whole chapter. That is a sad commentary, but it is what it is and if you read this chapter carefully, you can avoid 99% of the scams out there today.

If there is one chapter I want you to read carefully and then reread, it's this one. After all, what good is it to make sound financial decisions and then watch the fruits of your labor go up in smoke? What I see today is a lawless society that is out of control on so many fronts, especially with the proliferation of technology! Let's spend some time talking about the various kinds of scams I've come across during my career and discuss what you can do to steer clear of these expensive hoaxes—what you don't know can really hurt you.

Wire Scams

$1.4 million gone in a nanosecond. Yes, I've watched fraud on that scale happen in the blink of an eye, and when it happens it's terrible for everyone involved. We've all gotten those emails from a Prince of Botswana who offers you a return on your investment in sky-high multiples if only you'll wire money now so he can inherit his royal fortune. These emails contain little detail beyond how and where to wire your money!

At Bank of America, we had a very strict protocol to test the legitimacy of a wire request—we asked the client to verify the wire instructions on a recorded line. The problem with an email containing wire instructions is it can easily be intercepted by bad people who change the bank account number so the crooks obtain your funds and you are left holding the bag—an empty one at that!

Think about this for a second. You're ready to close escrow on your dream home and you wire a substantial amount of money to the escrow company. Unfortunately, the company never receives your funds because the wire winds up going to Timbuktu. Not only do you lose your money but, obviously, you also do not close escrow, so you lose the dream house, too. If this happens, it needs to be figured out posthaste because the clock is ticking, and the funds can only be returned to you if the fraud is detected early in the process.

I remember hearing about a client who, supposedly, had sent an email to his advisor, asking for a wire to be completed. The client was out of the country, so the advisor contacted the wife to verify the legitimacy of the wire. Without calling her husband, she said the wire was okay. The wire was $1.4 million. Imagine the shock on both of their faces when the husband returned home, the wife mentioned the wire to him, and he told her he had not sent wire instructions to their advisor.

By that time, unfortunately, too much time had elapsed, so the return of the wire was impossible. I never heard what the final outcome was, and I'm not sure I want to, but someone suffered a major loss! The bottom line is if you are going to wire money anywhere for anything, double check the wire instructions from your receiving party and make sure your bank has the correct wire instructions as well. *And more than anything else,* communicate with your spouse about all major financial transactions!

Although I've been extremely careful and I'm a professional wealth manager, even I have been a victim of fraud. My first experience was with my debit card being compromised at our local grocery store. Not pleasant, to say the least. My credit card has also been hacked around five times in the last 15 years. And I've been ripped off when purchasing items on the Internet and not being reimbursed when I returned the item because it was not as advertised. In the last case, I had ordered pillows and wished to return them, only to find out that they had to be shipped to Lithuania and the cost of shipping exceeded the cost of purchasing them in the first place. What a grift.

The first and most fundamental piece of advice I will give you is to monitor your bank account and credit cards at least every other day to verify that all charges are correct. If they aren't, contact your bank immediately and obtain a new card. You may even have to change your bank account number just to be on the safe side. But by all means, monitor your bank accounts and be wary of buying items online from unknown vendors. Personally, my wife and I have had great experiences with Amazon.

Beware of the Trojan Horse

Just about every home in America has a Trojan Horse in it. By this I mean you have an object in your home that can be perilous to your financial well-being. And what is this, you ask? It's your computer.

With all of a computer's benefits, it also presents some peril if you are not careful. Here are three suggestions for your consideration.

1. Be very careful with unsolicited emails, especially those that ask for personal information such as credit card information. A perfect example is one we receive almost daily from Sirius Radio telling us our subscription has expired and asking us to renew it using their email. Huh? Our subscription has not expired! Obviously, not from Sirius Radio itself!
2. Make sure you have an anti virus capability on your computer. This will at least provide some help in preventing bad actors from getting into your computer.
3. Never, ever, have your bank account viewing set up to populate the password automatically. If the thief can access your computer, they can steal all the money in your bank account, and you literally have no recourse except to report it to the authorities and hope you get your money back.

Financial Betrayal

Sadly, sometimes scams do not originate from outside the house but, in fact, are perpetrated from inside by those closest to us. Sometimes it's a family member or a friend or, even worse, someone we have trusted to manage our affairs with honesty and integrity. An example is when the person you would trust to write checks to pay your bills starts paying themselves!

I had a client who discovered the family confidant in charge of her books had been embezzling her funds. She discovered this quite by accident one day when she ordered a copy of a check that had been written and realized the bookkeeper had changed the payee to her own name. This set off a whole chain of events that led to the discovery of many more forged checks and a significant amount of stolen funds!

The irony was that the bookkeeper was a former employee of Security Pacific National Bank. I knew her because I worked at Security Pacific at the same time she did. She was intelligent, strong-willed, and apparently arrogant. I fervently believe she thought she would never get caught. She had worked for my client's father for many years, going to the house frequently to help keep their money affairs in order. Unfortunately, she lied to my client's father and then lied to my client about how much the father had been paying her. Then when the father passed away, the bookkeeper doubled her own pay.

I think the moral of the story is that you can trust, yes, but always, always verify that trust by monitoring what is happening with your funds. Be suspicious of people who suddenly become your best friend. Over the many years I worked in the financial services industry, I was shocked and disheartened to see and learn what people would do to take advantage of somebody else, even those closest to them. So, be on the lookout and be on guard to protect yourself, your loved ones, and your money.

The bottom line is you need to be extremely cautious and diligent when you hand over the reins to anyone who will handle, dispense, or even collect your money. It's advisable to use a CPA to audit your statements to make sure everything is on the up and up. I would include copies of your checks and confirmations of your investment transactions that will later be reflected on your statement. *But* the bottom line is *you* need to check to make sure everything is on the up and up. Review your statements, be sure to get copies of your written checks, and even ask someone you trust to look over your accounts.

Online Dating Scams: I'd Do Anything for Love

Dating online is a great new way technology helps you meet like-minded folks, but it also opens you up to a whole new world of scam potential. People are open and vulnerable when they are searching for love, and there are people you might run into on dating platforms who are aware of this. The people you connect with on the app may seem scrupulous and transparent, but they might not be what they seem.

I had a client who met a woman online who was 30 or 35 years his junior. When he introduced me to her, it was clear there was no affection there on her part, but I had a feeling she liked his considerable wealth just fine. The rubber hit the road when he called me one day in a frenzy, saying he was on his deathbed and urging me to wire \$500,000 to his girlfriend's account in Mexico. This set off the alarm bells in my head to put it mildly. After talking at length with our compliance people and with my client, I was able to reduce the wire request by 50%.

My client was not too happy about my precautionary move. In fact, my efforts to protect him went so badly that he told me if I ever tried something like that again he would pull his account. I only found out later that he had purchased a home for the girlfriend in Mexico for close to \$1 million, and then she dumped him. Those funds could never be re-patriated. So be forewarned. Don't let your heart lead you astray when it comes to your money.

I had another client who fell in love at first swipe. She had recently been widowed and was looking for love in all the wrong places. And she found it—or so she thought. The gentleman, if you can call him that, lived overseas and was singing love songs into her ear at long distance. He proposed in very short order, and she said "yes" without ever having met him in person. Imagine, they had not even *met!* Romeo's excuse for not meeting his Juliet was he could not travel because he had some medical issues. Next thing she knew, Romeo was asking for money to help cover his medical expenses. *Red flag!!* When someone on a dating website starts asking for money, run for the hills!

In 2023, it was estimated that online dating fraud had cost Americans $1.14 billion.[53] Authorities felt this number was way under-reported because of shame and embarrassment. The fraudsters' immediate goals are to (1) establish trust and (2) exploit hope from love from their victim.

I have heard many similar stories over the years, trust me. My advice is to go online and research the people you are considering getting involved with. If you dig deep enough, you can learn about a person's criminal background if one exists. Above all, insist on meeting the person at a neutral site like a restaurant or just for coffee. Avoid meeting in a bar because you never know if someone might slip you something. If the person is "not available" to meet locally, forget about them. That is warning flag number one. And, of course, warning flags numbers two, three, and four, are asking you for money.

I have seen the same process happen repeatedly with similar scams. These people are adept at sweet talking innocent people merely looking for romance. They will play their hand and bilk anyone and everyone they can out of their money. *Beware!*

I read an interesting story from our local paper, the Orange County Register, dated October 13, 2024. The article described the latest iteration of the romantic online con called "pig butchering." This is where a con man romances someone and then turns that romance into a get rich scheme using cryptocurrency as the bait. The con man shows the victim supposed proof it's real while all the time it is not! Please be careful out there, it is a jungle!

---

[53] Lesley Fair, " 'Love Stinks' – When a Scammer Is Involved," Federal Trade Commission, February 13, 2024, https://www.ftc.gov/business-guidance/blog/2024/02/love-stinks-when-scammer-involved.

Bank Hacks

In our new world, technology has certainly improved our lives, but there is most definitely a downside to automatic transfers and cash deposits. These conveniences have made it much easier for scammers to hack into your bank account. Again, check your bank account and credit cards periodically to make sure everything is in order. Be vigilant and stay in touch with your money.

I urge you never to have the bank app on your phone set to automatically access your bank account transactions without typing in the password. I strongly suggest you always log in into your bank app, because if someone sees you using your phone when you have just entered your password and later steals it, your bank account could be cleaned out in a matter of minutes.

Hard Sales and Advisor Scams

Some financial advisors will try to pressure you into investing in a product that benefits them more than it benefits you and they will want you to purchase it now! Urgency is a powerful tool because infusing a situation with urgency hijacks the time you need to do your due diligence. Watch out for phrases like, "Invest now or you'll be left out." There is never, ever, ever a need to invest right this very second. Investment is not something that should ever be done urgently or on the spur of the moment. If you're feeling pressure like that, excuse yourself and never speak to that advisor again.

One of the first things I'd tell a prospective client at our first meeting was they did not have to make any decisions during that meeting. I encouraged them to take the literature home and study the investments I was suggesting. Then I recommended they come back for a subsequent meeting with a list of questions I would be happy to answer. I encouraged them to sleep on it and talk to their family members or other professional people they associate with. And most of all, I encouraged investors to take their time and be comfortable with what I was proposing.

Hot Tips

Let's get this straight right from the top because there is a lot of misinformation about the idea of inside information. Once and for all, I am here to tell you as an expert authority that there is no such thing as a hot tip. In my 40 years as a financial advisor, I never came across the proverbial hot tip! Ever. And if you do come across an actual hot tip emerging from verified inside sources, it might be illegal.

Trust me on this one—if you act on inside information, you will more than likely get caught. This is particularly true if you invest a lot of money in something that is out of the norm for you—something outside of your normal investments. I guarantee you the Security Exchange Commission (SEC) monitors accounts and continuously looks for people who have traded on inside information. If you're caught, the consequences can be substantial.

Sky-High Yields and Returns

When you hear or read about something that offers a high yield or a high return, bear in mind the word "high" in this context means high risk. There is no such thing as high yield without a lot of risk. If somebody tells you that you can earn a big return on your money with low risk, they are not being honest with you. Steer clear. When you get greedy, you can fall easily for these kinds of appeals. It's wise to remember there are no free lunches and no return without risk. Risk and return exist in an inverse ratio. It's one of the physical laws of the financial universe and there are no exceptions.

Selling Away

Beyond the standard vehicles I have described for you thus far, there is a universe of financial products out there as numerous and varied as snowflakes. They can arrive as a separate investment like a stock or bond or they can be packaged like a mutual fund or ETF. Other packaged products include annuities, life insurance, limited partnerships, private equity deals, and on and on. There are all kinds of instruments and deals to be had out there, all with their own unique sets of considerations and pitfalls. So, investor beware!

When I first got into the investment world, a friend of mine showed me an investment that was being promoted by his CPA. My manager at the time was quick to ask how much due diligence the CPA had performed on that deal and whether it was even legitimate. Before we offered a client any investment product, we thoroughly vetted and reviewed it for any possible fraud and obviously checked its viability.

Here's the rub. When I worked at Merrill, all our investment products were thoroughly reviewed, and we only offered the best—the crème de la crème. If you were a money manager or offering limited real estate partnerships, wouldn't you want to have a large investment firm offering your product? The large firms get to choose the very best investment vehicles because the people who put these deals together need distribution to raise money. As a result, the larger the investment firm, the better the results in getting funds from investors at those large firms. But what about those vehicles that don't make it onto the platforms of large investment firms?

These more obscure investment vehicles get distributed to smaller firms, to CPAs, or, worse, to an investment advisor working for a large firm who offers these products to their clientele. This is a perfect example of selling away. In other words, the advisor is selling something that has not been reviewed or vetted by his or her firm. You must ask yourself, does that advisor have the wherewithal or expertise to understand and comprehend that investment vehicle? Or are they selling something away from their firm without really understanding the parameters of the financial instrument?

What's the motivation for an advisor to do this? Mostly, it comes down to money. When the advisor sells away, they keep the entire commission. If the advisor sells a product offered by the firm they work for, the commission is split, usually around 40% to the advisor and 60% to the firm. So, you can readily see the motivation for the advisor to sell away. However, this is a major compliance issue for advisors and if these rules are violated, it will usually—and hopefully—lead to termination.

Some years ago, I ran into an advisor who was offering products that were not on our platform. His client invested around $600,000 in these various products. When they went bad, the firm found out about the advisor's actions, terminated the advisor immediately, and the client was made 100% whole in terms of the original investments. So, stay alert! If your advisor offers you products, make sure they have been reviewed by the firm and your advisor is not "selling away" subpar investments.

If you are suspicious, call the branch manager and ask questions about the investment. You will know right away if the investment opportunity is on the platform and offered by the company you are working with.

Financial Advisor Fraud

Unfortunately, not all financial advisors are ethical. Some are outright dishonest. Advisors have been known to help themselves to money from a client's account, put it in their own account, and then doctor the statements sent to the client to disguise the transaction. Again, I urge you to review your statements online. In my opinion, it's extremely difficult for an advisor to change what is in the main computer of an investment firm. In addition, be forewarned that even the most seemingly honest advisor may not be. Remember that Bernie Madoff oversaw NASDAQ before he opened his own investment firm. That didn't end well for a lot of innocent clients. More recently, Sam Bankman-Fried bilked a lot of innocent investors with his cryptocurrency scheme.

Not to belabor the point, but one of the easiest ways to avoid financial advisor or investment company fraud is to deal only with the larger institutions. They have a myriad of safeguards in place to protect you, the investor. Believe me, I know because I worked for one of the largest investment firms in America. In addition, I would be leery of firms that have only a website address and no physical address. There is a comfort level in working with people directly rather than on a website.

Building Your Bulwark

There are two areas you need to look at before you hand your money over to an investment firm. First, take a long hard look at the investment firm itself. Second, take a long hard look at the advisor representing the firm. One of the most basic ways to check an investment firm is to see if they are a member of the Securities Investor Protection Corporation (SIPC). SIPC is designed to protect investors from fraud and safeguard them should the investment firm go bankrupt, as was the case with Lehman Brothers in 2008. Be aware, however, that there are limitations to the dollar amounts SIPC insures: $500,000 in investments and $250,000 in cash.[54]

Some firms take out additional insurance to cover the entire

54 "What SIPC Protects," SIPC, accessed September 28, 2024, https://www.sipc.org/for-investors/what-sipc-protects.

balance of all their investment accounts over $500,000. This is an additional expense borne by the firm. They should be able to provide proof they have gone this extra mile.

Bear in mind that SIPC does not cover losses due to market fluctuation. It only guarantees you will own your securities through thick and thin—you cannot lose them with SIPC around. If the firm you're considering doing business with does not have SIPC coverage, I strongly urge you to go elsewhere. Having this coverage is another indicator you are dealing with a reputable firm that cares about protecting its investors. You can find out whether a firm has SIPC coverage by going to the website at SIPC.org and checking under the tab, "Is your broker a SIPC member?"

Next, look at your investment advisor's background. This is easily done, as I have explained, by going to the FINRA website and typing your advisor's name into their BrokerCheck system. Be forewarned that if an advisor has been in the business for a long time, there could have been a complaint filed against them at some point. That is not the end of the world. I strongly suggest, however, that you read about the complaint and the advisor's response to it and judge for yourself whether it warrants looking elsewhere for another financial advisor.

If there are numerous complaints and monetary awards against the advisor, then obviously look elsewhere. Also, check to make sure the advisor is licensed to offer securities in the state where you reside. In addition, you should receive printed information from the advisor describing exactly what they are proposing to do for you. This may include a prospectus describing the investment(s) they are offering. That prospectus may be lengthy and written in legalese and not the easiest thing to understand. Nevertheless, it will provide essential information regarding the investment vehicle. There may be past results shown in the prospectus that look very positive and glowing—but remember history may not repeat itself.

One more bit of advice. Monitor your accounts! You can obtain a free copy of your credit report online at www.annualcreditreport.com or by calling toll free 1-877-322-8228. You may also purchase a copy of your credit report by contacting one of the three national credit reporting agencies listed below.

Equifax	Experian	TransUnion
1-800-685-1111	1-888-397-3742	1-800-888-4213
www.equifax.com	www.experian.com	www.transunion.com

When you receive your credit report, review it carefully. Look for accounts or creditor inquiries you did not initiate or do not recognize. Look for information such as your home address and Social Security number and verify their accuracy. If you see anything incorrect, call the credit reporting agency at the number listed above.

What to Do First When You've Been Conned

1. Document everything. Write down all the details you can remember about the transaction. Write down the company name, dates, and who you interacted with. In the case of an investment firm, note the advisors you worked with and their contact information, including their address, phone number, and website. Document all the information they gave you, a timeline of what happened, and file a police report that includes all the notes you've recorded.
2. If you've fallen in with a dishonest financial firm, I urge you to contact the Securities and Exchange Commission. They can be reached at 800-SEC-0330, or a complaint can be filed on their website at https://www.sec.gov/submit-tip-or-complaint. You should also contact FINRA at 301-590-6500. If you're a senior citizen, you can contact them at 844-574-3577. Their website address is http://www.finra.org/investors/investor-complaint-center. I would also contact your own

state's securities division. This can normally be found on your state's website.

Mistakes People Make with Their Money

Below are some of the common mistakes I've watched people make repeatedly with their money and wind up costing them in the end. These are the ways people, in a sense, scam themselves. I hope this will hone your prosperity mindset and help you avoid making some of these mistakes and learning the hard way.

Mistake #1: Lack of Knowledge

The first mistake the average investor makes is not having basic knowledge about what they are investing in. It's unfortunate finance is not a required subject in high school. If finance courses were provided, I think the average person would do a lot better when it comes to investing their funds and building wealth throughout the course of their lives.

Lack of knowledge can take many forms. Being able to converse with a financial advisor and having a basic level of understanding is extremely important—not only when it comes to investing your money but also in selecting the advisor who matches your financial style and vision. I hope by the time you finish reading this book you will be able to tell if your financial advisor's suggestions are worthy of your consideration or not.

I cannot begin to tell you how many people I've spoken with over the years who readily admit they have no knowledge about investing their funds at all—as in zilch, zero. Quite candidly, it makes the financial advisor's job that much more difficult, because the client is relying on the advisor's recommendations completely without a basis for providing customized input to guide the advisor's recommendations.

Mistake #2: Bypassing Due Diligence

I am sorry to tell you this, but not all investment firms are on the up and up. There are some illegitimate investment firms. I know, I'm sorry—I hate to burst your bubble but I'm telling you this so you understand that if you trust your money with an illegitimate investment firm, not only could your investments fail but your funds could literally be stolen from you. One of the best ways to minimize fraud is to deal with a larger firm with a well-established history like the Bank of Americas of the world, J. P. Morgan, and Morgan Stanley. These legacy institutions are going to give you an honest path to sound investment. These firms understand they have reputational risk, and they must act accordingly.

Where I've seen problems arise is often with the smaller firms that clear their own trades without much oversight or even any oversight at all. This is where fraud can and does exist. A perfect example of this is Bernie Madoff. He obviously did not use an outside firm to clear his trades because he wasn't making any trades at all. Thus, his investors were fleeced for many millions of dollars, and nobody was the wiser until the house came down. If you do choose to invest with a small firm, triple verify they're using a financial services company like Charles Schwab to clear their trades. In this way, you will have a lot more protection against fraud and getting ripped off.

Mistake #3: Relying on Someone Who Does Not Have a Strong Investment Background

Another big mistake the average investor makes is relying on someone else to help them with their investments. By this, I mean an outside person like a CPA or an attorney or the day trader who lives next door. Do not take advice from amateurs or experts from other fields. You wouldn't ask your mechanic to fix your high blood pressure, so do not ask a lawyer to strategize the market.

Mistake #4: Obsessing over Taxes

I've seen clients make money mistakes because they are too worried about their tax liability and overcompensate. I had a client who owned stock in a software company from San Jose called Gadzooks. He had earned a huge profit on the stock and was reluctant to sell it. I remember the stock had been approximately $75 per share and he did not want to sell because of the capital gains tax he had to pay. However, the stock price began to fall and ultimately the company went bankrupt. He lost way more money by not selling than he would have paid in capital gains taxes.

A good rule of thumb is to be aware of the potential taxes you must pay if you sell your stock or other investments, but do not make this the sole factor on which you base your investment decisions. Do not let taxes determine whether you sell a stock. Paying taxes is just a part of the investment process. Yes, I know it's painful, but you know what they say about death and taxes.

Mistake #5: Trying to Time the Market

Trust me, you can't. Investors always stumble when they try to make investments that rely on their ability to properly time the market. Simply put, this is when an investor tries to buy low and sell high on the margins with split-second timing. In my experience, this has hurt investors more than it has helped them. In general, there are more winning years in the marketplace than losing years. To wait for the market to go down and then buy in can be disastrous because you were not invested in the good years.

Over the course of my 40 years in the financial service sector, I've seen that the markets are up typically three out of every four years. When I started, the Dow Jones was at around 950 and today it is over 43,000. What I have seen over time is that, in general, there is no time like the present to invest funds. Obviously, I am not saying we haven't had tumultuous years in the marketplace—and perhaps sometimes by waiting you might do a lot better—but waiting offers no guarantees.

Along the same lines, you would be wise to consider dollar cost averaging. As an example, let's say you have $250,000 to invest. You could, on a systematic basis, invest $25,000 a month for the next 10 months. Thus, what happens is when the market goes down, you're buying more shares for that $25,000. And when the market goes up, you're buying fewer shares. This does not guarantee you will do better, but it may improve your odds.

Mistake #6: Greed

Unlike what Gordon Gecko told us in the movie *Wall Street*, greed is *not* good.[55] In fact, greed has led many investors down a primrose path to penury. A perfect example of greed going wrong is when you get a hot tip from a colleague telling you to buy a certain stock because the value is destined to go up. Your greed factor kicks in and says yes, do it. Buy! Buy! Buy! Then you find out later your hot tip wasn't so hot after all. Beware of the greed factor before you plunk your money down on an investment when your eyes have gotten bigger than your wallet. Invest with your brain, not with your unhealthier appetites.

---

[55] *Wall Street*, directed by Oliver Stone (1987; Twentieth Century Fox).

Mistake #7: There's a Sucker Born Every Day

Another big investment mistake I want to earmark for you is being sold a bill of goods by an unscrupulous advisor. Beware of the hard sell by an advisor. If you experience this, politely excuse yourself. Hard sell is a technique often used by an advisor who only thinks of themself.

Mistake #8: Failure to Communicate

People make the mistake of being secretive about their money and not communicating with the people directly connected to their financial situation. This can cause a real mess in the event of your death. Keep your spouse or partner informed about your investment accounts as well as money in general so they can step in if they need to.

Too often, when a client passed away, I found the surviving spouse or partner did not have a clue as to what their funds were invested in and where their money was. They did not know who to contact. I remember talking to one surviving spouse whose investment accounts totaled around $25 million, and she asked me, "Am I going to be, okay?" I thought to myself, "Absolutely!" She was a 75-year-old with no debt. Even if she spent $30,000 a month those funds would last 70 years. People need to communicate with their loved ones about their jointly held assets, just in case. Here are a few tips to avoid this communication breakdown.

One of the best pieces of advice I can give you is to communicate, communicate, and communicate with your spouse or trusted family member. The tips below are vital. I recommend you study and follow them to the letter!

Tips for Keeping Your Spouse Financially Informed

1. Review all your statements with your spouse or partner on a regular basis. Make sure they know exactly what the funds are invested in as well as where they're located. Most importantly, give them a contact name and phone number in case of an untimely death. You don't necessarily need to go line by line in detail about what each account contains, but rather it can be broken down to percentages of stocks, bonds, and money markets.
2. Make sure your spouse or partner meets with your advisor on a regular basis. In addition, make sure the advisor explains how to read an investment statement. Investment statements can be complicated and it's helpful to have some guidance. I recommend your advisor brief your partner not only on where the money is being invested (including current strategies) but also on which strategies are being implemented on a go-forward basis as you and your partner age.
3. Be sure to share your passwords and user IDs for the company websites where your funds are held with the individual(s) you trust—and keep them updated as your passwords change. I find using a little phonebook to store passwords works well, but I'm old school. One thing I can say about little notebooks, they can't be hacked. I suggest abbreviating the names of companies to mitigate potential problems should the book fall into the wrong hands.
4. Lastly, if possible, include your spouse or partner on the phone calls from your financial advisor. This will certainly prove unbelievably valuable as a positive learning experience for both of you and will keep you and your partner on the same page. Plus, if anything should happen to one of you, the other will know exactly what to do.

The point is not to make your spouse or partner an investment expert—it's to make sure they will not have any further discomfort should something happen to you. I cannot begin to tell you how many times I have spoken to a surviving spouse or partner and—compounding an already bad situation—found they now have money worries! They did not have a clue what the money was invested in or a comfort level in knowing they had enough money. So, a word to the wise—keep your spouse or partner well-informed as to what the money is invested in, where it is, and who to contact.

Don't Shortchange Yourself

One client of mine stands out as the worst example I have ever witnessed of what can happen when you listen to bad advice. This client wound up losing literally everything because he did not understand the dangerous way he was thinking about his wealth or question the motives of his wealth advisors.

The first step he took toward disaster was deciding to rely on his CPA as a financial advisor. In the first place, CPAs are not investment advisors. They know about accounting, not investing. So that was mistake number one. Mistake number two was this CPA was extremely aggressive. My client was timid, even hesitant at times, and he was letting his CPA run right over him. The advisor wanted his investments to make as much money as possible as quickly as possible and he was pushing my client to keep up. The advisor decided the best way to realize the returns he was looking for was in shorting technology stocks. He convinced my client to enter a world he completely did not understand.

Before I go any further, for those of you who haven't seen *The Big Short*, I should explain a little bit about what it means to short a stock. Most people understand the concept of buying a stock at a low price and selling it later at a higher price to garner a profit. It's the classic buy low and sell high method of investing. What most people do not realize, however, is you can flip-flop the process. In other words, if you have the ability and are approved by the financial service firm you are working with, you can sell stock you don't even own and then hold that position, betting the price of the stock will go down instead of up so you can earn a profit from the shareholder's loss.

Sounds kind of crazy, doesn't it? That's because it is, as far as I'm concerned. It's all too daring and dubious for this conservative advisor. I like win/win scenarios and I'm not big on profiting from somebody else's loss. While technically legal, shorting stocks is a dicey affair I have steered away from in my career for very good reason. Just for the record though, this is how a short works.

A short begins when a firm borrows stock from another client's account and allows you to sell the stock today at the share value it holds at that moment. At some point, if the stock moves to a lower price, you can then buy the stock back at the lower price and earn a profit. The problem with this concept is you can set yourself up for unlimited trading losses, meaning *losing* everything and then some if things don't go your way. Bear in mind the price of a stock can theoretically can move up and up, leading to unlimited losses, whereas if you purchase a stock, your downside risk is the stock going to zero.

I worked with an elderly couple I adored, let's call them Sam and Ethel. They were a delightful pair, both had Hollywood movie industry ties dating to the early 1940s. Sam was a writer. Ethel had been a glamorous actress and even appeared opposite a young and dashing Ronald Reagan in *Knute Rockne, All American.* You might remember the famous saying from the movie: "Win just one for the Gipper."[56]

---

[56] *Knute Rockne, All American,* directed by Lloyd Bacon and William K. Howard (1940; Turner Entertainment Co.).

They got married at PickFair, the home of Douglas Fairbanks and Mary Pickford, who were both giant silent screen movie stars about a thousand years ago.[57] Ethel, in fact, was the niece of Mary Pickford. Sadly, Sam passed away in early 1998 and Ethel handed over the duties of the trust to her son, Joseph.

Ethel and Sam had maintained a very conservative portfolio at our bank. They had invested in municipal bonds and blue-chip stocks back in the mid-1980s and continued to do so through the 90s. They had good returns on their accounts and the stock market had moved in their favor. After Sam passed away in 1998, their son Joseph took over the responsibility for managing the investment account which was of a respectable size and had been taking care of the two of them.

I met Joseph for the first time in 1998. We got along well. He was around my own age, only about seven years or so older, and he was a screenwriter who also had ties with old Hollywood. They are a unique and a distinct breed, old Hollywood royalty. He drove to Newport Beach to deliver the stock certificates from his parents and afterward, we walked across the street to Fashion Island to have lunch at Chimayo. We shared our worries as homeowners and bonded over our mistrust of modern disruption. He was a great lunch companion. He had worked on some scripts for the Pink Panther series and had written a movie for Hallmark, but largely he had lived a privileged life thanks to the legacy wealth of his Hollywood royal family.

We seemed to have so much to talk about though we had few things in common. But we were both young men learning to grapple with the responsibilities of home ownership which can be challenging. We bonded over home ownership like brothers. Remodeling is hell. I looked forward to working with him. Even during that first

57 "The Legendary PickFair Estate," Eden, accessed September 28, 2024, https://www.eden.com/real-estate/the-legendary-pickfair-estate/.

meeting, however, I got the distinct impression he was in a little over his head with his parents' estate. He seemed brand new to the world of investments. Then I got a good scare when he told me over lunch one day he was letting his CPA give him investment advice.

I decided it would be a good idea to meet with his CPA, compare notes, and give myself the opportunity to size this guy up. So, I drove to Century City to meet this brilliant investment CPA, hoping we might formulate some strategies on how to manage the account together. Like I said, I enjoy a win/win scenario whenever possible. The account at that time was valued at around $3.5 million and was composed of $2 million in treasuries, $1 million in long-term California municipal bonds and around $500,000 in stocks. A very balanced, conservative portfolio. Their son was a different matter entirely, as we are about to see. Balance and equilibrium are not the words that spring to mind when I think back on Joseph.

This CPA had worked with Sam and Ethel for a long time and with Joseph for several years before he took over his parents' trust. The CPA, let's call him Svengali, seemed intelligent, informed, articulate, and very, very, *very* sure of himself. One might even say cocky, and I don't really like that in an advisor. Nobody wants a cocky advisor, trust me. We want our advisors to be sober and dressed in blue or gray suits.

I am suspicious of anyone who speaks like an expert on subjects they know precious little about. Svengali was not a financial advisor—he was an accountant, which is a vastly different skill set. And yet here he was, signing on as advisor and telling poor, inexperienced Joseph what to do with his money. And Joseph followed the leader. I found the whole situation troubling and uncomfortable.

I remember driving home after the meeting and thinking to myself that this would be the first CPA I ever worked with who I would learn something from. I realized later this was quite visionary on my part. *But I had absolutely no idea that what I would learn would result in the tragic set of events I was about to witness.*

His advice at that point was for my client to invest in stocks that had "lost momentum." This was code for shorting stocks—particularly in the technology sector—that would deliver big profits in record time. A little fishy perhaps? I thought so too. In my view, it's never a good sign when somebody is looking to get rich quick, especially when that somebody is both your CPA and your investment advisor. This was definitely not his parents' conservative and balanced investment philosophy anymore.

Despite my general skepticism of anybody who promises you the moon, Joseph would not pump the brakes. He seemed entranced with Svengali's pie in the sky outlook, and the first order of business on Svengali's list was to tell Joseph to sell all the stock his parents had held in certificate form for decades. Shortly thereafter, I looked on horrified as all those legacy stocks his parents had long held so carefully and judiciously were put on the block.

These were all blue-chip American companies they were selling. Top shelf, top quality investments with returns as stable and predictable as rain in the springtime, just gone with the wind. Poof. This move to liquidate my client made me uncomfortable to say the least, but there was nothing I could do because I was not the investment advisor. Svengali was. All I could do was look on as Joseph began to slide down a very slippery slope.

As time marched forward, it became apparent the technology stocks were not going in the right direction for Joseph and Svengali. The stocks were becoming overpriced and a bubble was forming. It seemed like any company that ended in dot-com was off to the races and moving toward higher prices every day. Nobody could understand why, especially not Svengali. I remember all too well the mantra at that time was, "Earnings do not matter." Whenever you hear somebody say something like that to you, run for your life. It was difficult and unexplored for even the most seasoned advisor, and Svengali was in over his head with Joseph's money.

I remember Warren Buffett saying he did not understand technology stocks at all.[58] Even the great Warren Buffett did not understand how stock prices could be so inflated when the companies themselves were not making any money and there was no actual value driving valuations. Welcome to the dot-com nineties, where money and value were beside the point and people were selling vaporware for billions.

Joseph's overly self-confident Svengali CPA then decided to make money in this kind of a market, he needed to begin shorting technology stocks pronto. That's another thing to look out for—never let an advisor rush you into any investment idea. I remember thinking to myself that Joseph was making a high-risk bet with a high-pressure advisor, and I could feel he was headed for a cliff.

On the other hand, in my opinion, technology stocks had formed a bubble and if that bubble popped, stock prices would typically drop precipitously and offer a huge profit for my client. Interestingly, by that point I had been in the investment world for 16 years and this was the first time I'd ever had a client request to sell stocks short. So, I would have been the first to admit I was no expert. It just wasn't my cup of tea. Who was I to intervene? Worse, what if I said something and the CPA turned out to be right?

So, we were off to the races and my client started shorting tech stocks. The problem was, as if often the case in a fluid market, his timing was off. Honestly, timing the market properly is next to

---

58 Nick Baker and Katherine Chiglinsky, "Warren Buffett Once Said He Didn't Invest in Tech Stocks Because He Didn't Understand Them—He Might Have Been Right," Financial Post, January 3, 2019, https://financialpost.com/investing/buffetts-apple-losses-make-his-track-record-in-tech-even-worse.

impossible, even for professionals. There's very little margin for error. Your timing must be exactly right, down to the second, or you're dead. And when you take such a huge amount of risk and short a stock, banking on huge returns, you better know what you are doing—including getting your timing right—or you're going to get your clock cleaned.

Looking back, if Svengali and Joseph had waited until March of 2000 and then shorted the technology stocks, they could have quadrupled my client's money as the tech-heavy NASDAQ went from around 5,000 to 1,139 by October of 2002.

Unfortunately for Joseph, while the plan was great in theory, in practice it was a total bust. Timing wasn't just off by a day or a week but a full year and a half. Svengali was way too early in making his prediction about the bubble bursting, and technology stocks just continued to appreciate. For me, it looked like this could build into a full-blown financial disaster for Joseph.

As Joseph's shorted tech stocks continued to rise in price, we were now getting margin calls, which is a demand from a bank for additional capital when an account runs low on funds. I do not believe in using margin calls to buy or sell stocks because it compounds your risk. It's like having an ATM card at a casino when you're losing at craps. When you're shorting stocks, however, a margin account is required. You must have an open tab. It can't be avoided. When a margin call is issued to bring the equity in the account to the required minimum, the client only has a couple of options: they can close out the position, meaning they can buy, or sell, or they can deposit more money or securities into their account to maintain their position.

All through that long and terrible year, Joseph kept getting margin calls, and by Christmas of 1998, my client's account was decimated. He then transferred his Dean Witter account to us and asked us to make even more short sales. By the end of December, he had a value of around $1.3 million left in the account. Good, I thought, at least the December statement will look somewhat decent. At least he's not broke!

Just one month later, I remember the exact date—it was Friday, January 8, 1999. My client called and when I answered he did not say hello but mumbled my name in a lifeless monotone. "Frank," he said, his voice thick with regret, "I'm broke. It's my mistake. I was wrong, I've lost everything and it's all my fault." I didn't know what to say to him at that moment. It wasn't a surprise I guess, but still I was stunned. I honestly did not know how to comfort him. He was right. He was ruined. I asked him to explain what had happened, but he couldn't spit out anything but his final instructions to me.

"Leave the two positions on the table," he told me. "I know I may have to take money out of checking to cover the losses. I still have a million dollars, so Mom's okay, I'll be okay." And then he hung up.

I felt so terrible for him. I couldn't imagine absorbing that kind of a loss. He had lost everything his parents had managed to save over their entire lifetimes. His lifestyle would never be the same and neither would his mother who was still alive at that point.

I had been hoping and praying the CPA's strategy would ultimately prove my instincts wrong and make a fortune for my client, but it was not to be. In January of 1999, the technology stocks continued to appreciate. On January 11, 1999, his two remaining short investments closed up—Lycos at 39.25% and InfoSeek at 32.63%. It was unbelievable appreciation in just *one* day, and now my client was ruined!

On that awful Monday, January 11, it was over. We could no longer do any trading because there was no remaining equity in my client's account to satisfy the margin calls. He could not make any more bad bets. Or any good ones either. He'd started with account at over $3.5 million, now he was half a million in debt to our bank.

And it had all happened in less than a year!

Sadly, it got even worse from there. I tried calling my client repeatedly over the days and weeks following this fall, but I never was able to reach him. Finally, someone picked up at his home and informed me he was not doing well and would not be home for some time. I could not help wondering what the heck happened. Where was he? He couldn't have passed away in his sleep—he was only 54. My assistant called various hospitals in the area and finally found him at Cedars Sinai in West Los Angeles. I found out later he had attempted suicide.

Fast forward three years and we have now entered arbitration over the loss. On February 3, 2002, I made my way to a swanky hotel in Santa Monica and had dinner with the attorneys representing myself and the bank. I arrived in the middle of the Super Bowl when Tom Brady won his first Super Bowl ring beating the St. Louis Rams. On Monday morning, the arbitration hearing started. There was a panel of three arbitrators in the room, my client's attorneys and the attorneys representing myself and my firm were present. Trust me on this one, arbitration is not something you want to go through voluntarily. It's grueling, painful, boring, and long. Especially in this case. But whenever somebody loses that much money that quickly, there will always be an arbitration hearing, especially when the client now owed us money!

I did see Joseph at the arbitration. We said hello and exchanged pleasantries. I was glad to see he was out of the hospital and looking well and I was surprised at how courteous and cordial he was toward me. I couldn't help but wonder—if the roles were reversed, how would I be treating him? Of course, what happened was not my fault, but I was someone who watched on helplessly while he tossed away a fortune.

Joseph told me he was feeling better, although his wife had

divorced him and he only had supervised visitation with his children. But he was on the mend, he said, and I had to admit he did look far healthier than the last time I'd seen him. Thank God for small mercies! I learned that Svengali had declared bankruptcy. Could not have happened to a nicer guy.

How did all this happen? Well, at our firm in 1998, all trades on the equity side had to be unsolicited. This is because we had no research team that allowed us to give informed opinions to the client about the stock market in general and stocks the client either wanted to buy or sell. We could only solicit fixed income, mutual funds, and annuities. We were strictly order takers when it came to placing equity trades. This changed long ago, thank goodness, but not soon enough for Joseph.

When my client expressed a desire to short technology stocks, it became a very gray area in terms of my ability to stop him. The obvious problem was no one really knew how those trades would work out. If we stopped him and the market began to move lower, we would have had a major liability on our hands because we would have cost him a fortune. We would have prevented the client from profiting from his existing positions and the ability to make a profit on potential future trades. I was literally helpless to stop the avalanche.

I've chosen to tell this story because it taught me this golden rule about money: Do not take advice from amateurs, strangers, friends, or neighbors. Find a professional who shares your risk tolerance and investment style, who understands your goals and what you are hoping to accomplish over the course of your financial life. And don't pair up with somebody, like my poor client, who's looking to get rich quick on your dime.

Bottom line—don't be a sucker. Do not take any wooden nickels. Be forewarned that many financial advisors are super slick salespeople and not really advisors at all. When you start feeling pressure from that advisor to take their recommendations, whether you want to or not, learn to say no and go elsewhere.

Golden Strategies

1. Always be skeptical of being asked for money from unsolicited emails especially when you did not initiate the purchase.
2. Be skeptical of *any* unsolicited emails, especially those asking for a renewal for a club membership or subscription. Call the company with a phone number you've verified separately and confirm the authenticity of the request. In fact, unless I am definitely interested in the email, I delete it.
3. Check your bank account *and* your investment account weekly at the very minimum. I check mine daily. Be on the lookout for any unauthorized activity.
4. Be leery of receiving investment advice from CPAs and attorneys.
5. Lastly, consider whether a recommended investment makes sense to you *and* whether you fully understand it.

Workshop Topics

1. On your computer, type in the name of the county or city where you live and add two words—investor fraud. I did this by typing in Orange County Investor Fraud and was a bit startled at what I found. Lots of bad people out there. I have known for years that Orange County has more than its fair share of fraud, but, oh my! The point is to get an understanding of what the fraudsters are doing so you don't fall prey to them!
2. My biggest concern for you is to make sure you take an *active* role in dealing with your investments. That means reviewing

your statements monthly and monitoring your account on your computer. Get into the habit of doing this and asking for help if you don't fully comprehend what is going on!

GOLDEN RULE 7

BEWARE THE EIGHT PITFALLS OF MONEY MISMANAGEMENT

It's a Jungle Out There

Pitfall 1: Do *Not* Borrow to Make Investments

Unless you're a super savvy investor, I highly recommend you not borrow money to make your investments. If somebody says, "Hey I've got a hot tip," first, there's no such thing that's legal. Second, even if it is a prime opportunity, if you don't have the cash liquid and discretionary, then you don't make the investment. The problem with borrowing to invest is it magnifies both your gains and losses and exposes you to a lot of unnecessary risk.

To give you an example, say you wanted to purchase 100 shares of a stock that was selling for $1,000, then your total investment would be $100,000. Now if you were to purchase that same stock on margin—which is the securities world's way of saying you are borrowing to make your investment—you would only have to put up $50,000 to make that investment. So, if the stock appreciated in price to $150,000 you would have doubled your money.

Conversely, if the stock price dropped to $500, you would have lost your entire initial investment. Compare this to purchasing the same stock and paying the entire amount of the transaction. Yes, your upside would be less, assuming the security appreciated in value but, given the risks in the stock market, your downside would also be considerably less. I am convinced that the risk/reward ratio for getting more bang for your buck, given the risk, is not worth it.

Another thing to consider is when you borrow money to make investments, you pay interest on the borrowed amount. Margin rates are very expensive! To put that into perspective, they are around double what you would pay for a home loan. What this means is your investment will have to appreciate by more than that to begin to make money. That is not an easy task!

In addition, if the equity in your account is not sufficient, you will receive a margin call. What this means in simple terms is you do not have enough money in the account to warrant the risk your investment firm is taking by allowing you to buy on margin. Also, there are only three ways to satisfy a margin call. First, if the margin call is for $10,000 you must sell $20,000 of securities to meet that call. That's because you must double the number of securities you have to sell to meet the margin call. Second, you can always bring in additional cash to the account to shore up the equity to meet the margin requirements. And third, you can bring in additional securities to shore up the equity in the account.

I remember early on in my career I worked with a gentleman who was quite confident about investing in technology-related stocks. This would have been around 1983. He also wanted to buy these with borrowed funds (margin) to try to get more bang for the buck.

Unfortunately, his timing was not too great, and he had numerous margin calls. And to compound things, he took off for Hawaii on vacation and I did not have a number at which to reach him. So, when the margin calls came through, I had to sell portions of his positions to meet the calls. That was the absolute worst time to be selling because the stock prices were down, which was what created the margin call in the first place. Buying on margin worked against my client and I've never recommended buying securities that way.

I will never forget talking to Leo Arena about purchasing securities on margin. You remember Leo, my most memorable client who I told you about in detail in chapter 1. One of his favorite sayings was, "cash and carry." He was dead set against buying securities on margin and I endorse his thinking 100%.

Pitfall #2: Avoid IPOs

IPO stands for Initial Public Offering, a means whereby corporations sell stock to raise money for general corporate purposes. Over the past many years there's been a frenzy in terms of people buying IPOs as they came out. Many people have profited from these offerings—however, I do not recommend them for you. I firmly believe in investing in proven ideas and, when it comes to equity investing, that means investing in companies with a long track record.

Initial means just that. An IPO is typically a new company that wants to raise funds, and a good portion of those funds go to the owner(s). Investing in this manner can be profitable, but unless you have the knowledge to really understand the pros and cons of this investment, I would stay away. Also, the underwriters are going to price the stock as high as possible, which may limit the upside and, yes, I have seen companies that went public eventually go bankrupt despite the due diligence of the underwriters. Now if you are a sophisticated investor and know the nuances of the IPO market, then investing in IPOs could prove profitable. Just remember you are investing in a company that does not have a long track record.

Pitfall #3: Avoid Chasing Return

You are doing yourself a horrible disservice if you invest money based on looking in the rearview mirror. By this I mean buying a mutual fund or ETF or investing in a separately managed account where recent returns have been spectacular. You should only be buying or investing in proven strategies that have an existing track record of at least 10 years. I am all too aware of some of the returns on various mutual funds and ETFs that had spectacular returns during Covid. If you invested in those portfolios and stayed with them for the next several years, returns were extremely positive and ultimately went extremely negative.

If you look at the ETF with the ticker symbol ARKK, this fund had spectacular returns in 2019 and 2020. In 2019 it was up 35.73% and in 2020 it was up an amazing 152%. However, in 2021 it was down 23.35% and in 2022, it was down 67%. In 2023 it was up 67%.[59] Talk about volatility! Imagine if you invested at the beginning of 2021—you would have been down 80% by the end of 2022!

I also remember investors chasing the technology bubble in the mid and late 90s, when any company that ended in dot-com performed well—until it didn't. There were so many dot-coms that none of us could keep track of them all. Looking back, the irony was so many of them were simply modern mail-order companies. When I was a child, our family used to receive the Sears Christmas catalog. My parents would complete the order blank, enclose a check, and drop the envelope in the mail. The dot-coms were like that, but

[59] "Performance," ARKK, accessed September 29, 2024, https://www.ark-funds.com/funds/arkk.

the merchandise was posted online, and you completed your online order and/or you called the company directly. The major difference was there was no longer a catalog available. It's my firm belief that this was not some revolutionary technology, rather just modern mail-order. My skepticism proved correct when a lot of the dot-coms went out of business.

Pitfall #4: Avoid Limited Partnerships

Limited partnerships[60] can take the form of many distinct types of investments and many of them feel a little risky to me. The problem I have with limited partnerships is if things start to go bad, your ability to withdraw funds from the partnership can be extremely limited—if it exists at all. I remember offering oil and gas drilling partnerships when I was at Smith Barney. Suffice to say the exploration of oil and gas is very risky at best. To put it mildly, success is not 100%. It seems obvious now but, in general, my experiences with limited partnerships have not been positive.

Pitfall #5: Avoid High-Yield Bond Funds[61]

I would advise staying away from high-yielding anything and this is particularly true when it comes to high-yield bond funds. These can best be described as junk bonds. While the yield will certainly be higher than that of a higher-credit quality portfolio, all it takes is for a couple of the bonds in the fund to default and your overall total return will be significantly less than if you had invested in a higher

[60] Evan Tarver, "Limited Partnership (LP): What It Is, Pros and Cons, How to Form One," Investopedia, last modified June 25, 2024, https://www.investopedia.com/terms/l/limitedpartnership.asp.

[61] James Chen, "High-Yield Bond: Definition, Types, and How to Invest," Investopedia, last modified August 11, 2023, https://www.investopedia.com/terms/h/high_yield_bond.asp.

quality bond portfolio in the first place.

Another caveat is a high-yield bond portfolio valuation will be in tandem with the economy. This is totally the opposite of how high-quality bond prices move. When the economy was in turmoil, a high-yield portfolio moved lower because the lower credit rated companies were much more susceptible to default. Ironically, given that interest rates move lower when times are challenging, the high-quality portfolio will move higher in price because interest typically moves lower. What I found over the years is high-yield bond portfolios are subject more to economic risk than interest-rate risk. When the economy slows down, you will find that a high-yield bond portfolio performed very poorly. I learned this the hard way early in my career and stayed away from this type of investment ever since.

Pitfall #6: Avoid Investing in Any One Industry or Any Country

In 1968 a song was released entitled "One." It was written by Harry Nilsson, though it is better known for its cover version performed by Three Dog Night. The first line of the lyrics contained the phrase: "the loneliest number." So, you may be asking yourself—why in the world am I bringing up Harry Nilsson and how does the number one apply to the art of investing? Well, in investing, you will learn Harry was right. One really is the loneliest number when it comes to your finances.

To help you understand why you should keep Harry's song in mind, I'll give you three stories about clients who got caught with that unlucky number that illustrate my point. The first client owned only one stock, which sometimes did very well for him. The stock hit an all-time high of $55.08 on November 30, 2006. My client was wearing rings on his fingers and bells on his toes during his glory days. By the end of 2008 though, that same lonely stock was trading for around $33. It reached a low of $3.63 on March 2, 2009. That was during the Great Recession, which is long behind us now and with any luck will never happen again.

From September 28, 2007, until September 26, 2008, the common stock was paying $0.64 per share per quarter. By March 27, 2009, the dividend amount dropped to one cent per share per quarter and was not raised until September 26, 2014, when it was then five cents per share per quarter. Today, the dividend amount is $0.24 per share per quarter. So, if you had all your funds in that particular stock and you purchased it in 2006, it's doubtful your investment is worth what you started with even though it's been nearly 17 years.

If you are going to invest in the stock market, you need to own not just one but a recommended average of at least 20 different stocks. Remember that not every stock has to appreciate in price to get a positive return, just the majority. Even if you invest with the best manager in the world, they will have some losing positions in their portfolio. Diversifying is easily accomplished via a separately managed account or a mutual fund or an ETF. I will explore those ownership concepts in more detail later in the book.

Another perfect example of a lonely number one was my client who owned a huge position in one of our local banks in Southern California. I can remember our compliance department sending him a letter every so often warning him of the perils of having just one stock in his investment account. If they went bankrupt and we had not warned him, we could have had a major liability on our hands. While he did have other investments, particularly in real estate, his investment account with me was just the one. That concept can really come back to bite you if that one bank fails or your one stock goes off the rails. In 2023 we did experience some significant bank failures. One of those was First Republic, which I felt was a reasonably well-run bank until it wasn't. The same rule applies over and over again. Diversify, diversify, diversify!

Lastly, I had a client who was Chinese American and wanted to invest in China's stock market. I showed him a mutual fund that was devoted to investing in Chinese stocks. He invested in it and unfortunately the volatility up and down was horrible. This can also be true if you invest in just one industry. Despite all the political turmoil, I feel quite strongly that the best country to invest in is the good ol' United States of America!

The bottom line is you want to avoid the number one when it comes to investing. Always, *always* have your funds invested in different instruments. If you have a stock portfolio it should include at least 20 to 30 companies, and if you have a bond portfolio it should include at least five different issues.

Pitfall #7: Avoid Annuities

I have said it before and I'll say it again for emphasis—I do not like annuities. Number one, when you buy an annuity, you are faced with surrender fees. While most annuities allow you to withdraw 10% of your money invested in the first year and years thereafter without a fee, many of them have a steep surrender penalty. This applies to a withdrawal of more than 10% of the original principal invested. The fees may be as high as 7% and gradually go down over the next five to 10 years. So, liquidity is challenging, to put it mildly. An internal fee within the annuity can also be extremely high, so make sure you understand up front what that fee is! Remember the fees you're paying will directly affect your returns. Have you ever read a prospectus from an annuity company? They are written in unintelligible legalese that is not at all easy to understand, even for me—and I'm a professional.

Also, if the financial advisor you are talking to suggests you buy an annuity particularly early in the conversation, I would politely excuse myself and run for the door. Obviously, that advisor is looking out for his or her interests and not yours. Be aware that annuities are one of the highest commission products paid to the advisor available today.

Pitfall #8: Avoid Alternative Investments

Alternative investments can take many diverse forms. These investments may include such things as venture capital, commodities, hedge funds, private equity, real estate, and even digital currencies. To be successful in this type of investment, you need some of the same attributes as you do when investing in equities. These include time, great street smarts for evaluating the investment and the risk tolerance in the first place, and enough reserves to make sure you won't need those funds for a long time. If you are interested in an investment, make sure you discuss your decision at length with your advisor. Learn exactly what it takes to get out of the investment if and when it terminates. Stocks, bonds, mutual funds, and ETFs are always liquid, and your funds are available to you the next business day. You may not like the value, but they do offer easy access to your principle.

Alternative investments are typically aimed at higher net worth clientele. Again, I am not too enthusiastic given the limited liquidity features and complicated structures that often involve internal fees and so on. There are better investments elsewhere. Again, as with IPOs, if you are a sophisticated investor and fully understand the risks associated with alternative investments—including liquidity features, capital calls, and on and on—then and only then would I recommend alternative investing for you.

Golden Strategies

1. KISS. How many times have you heard the phrase Keep It Simple Stupid? It certainly applies to investing. I vividly remember studying and trying to understand Collateralized Mortgage Obligations (CMOs) before the mortgage meltdown in 2008 and 2009. Try as I might, I could not figure out this type of investment and I never offered them to any of my clients. Thank goodness, because those investments did not end well, to say the least.
2. Always look for a track record. It could be from a mutual fund or managed account or other investments. Make sure there is some history behind your investment strategy.
3. Because this book is aimed at the non-professional investor, I recommend avoiding the pitfalls of certain investments I've outlined in this chapter.
4. I have found that less than 1% of the population is really sophisticated enough when it comes to investing. Don't go it alone.

Workshop Topics

1. Ask an insurance agent for a brochure on a fixed annuity and a variable annuity along with the accompanying prospectus. Learn about the main difference between the two, namely that the fixed annuity has a fixed interest rate for a period of time and will adjust periodically, while the variable annuity will typically be tied to the returns in the stock market. Also, make sure you find the fee structure in the prospectus. It will more than likely surprise you.
2. See if you can obtain a prospectus for an IPO from an advisor or a friend who buys IPOs. Ask yourself whether this

company will fly, will it succeed? For my readers, I recommend only investments that have a track record. Given that an IPO means a company is going public—issuing stock—they do *not* have a track record.

3. Compare the returns of good ol' U.S. companies with those of overseas companies. This is easily accomplished by searching for the best mutual funds in the international arena versus funds that only invest in America and will provide some ticker symbols you can use on the Morningstar.com website. Ticker symbols provide a means for you to obtain current quotes and research particular companies, mutual funds, or ETFs. I think you will see why I like investing in the U.S. versus overseas.

GOLDEN RULE 8

YOUR WEALTH IS BIGGER THAN YOUR BOTTOM LINE

Using Your Money to Help Others and Solve Problems in the World

There is a responsibility that comes with financial success and that is to enrich the society that has nurtured you and give back to those less fortunate than you. That is certainly true given the times we are currently living in. While money will not solve all the problems we face, it can go a long way toward helping our fellow human beings and our planet. Find a way to give back that feels right for you, your awareness, your time, and your fortune.

I wrote this book as my way to give back to society. Most Americans do not have a clue about how to save or how to invest their hard-earned money, but if they follow the golden rules outlined in this book, they will do infinitely better and enjoy better lives. This brings me great joy, knowing that in some small way, I will have made somebody else's road a little bit easier. That especially applies to the 60 million or so people who have the benefit of a 401(k). Here again, there is a major disconnect between investment knowledge and securing good returns for a retirement free of money worries. I am pledging to give all the money I make from this book to worthy causes. I hope there will be a nice sum to give to people in need.

Interestingly, if I sell 1,000 books or 1,000,000 books, it will not change my life one bit. Thankfully, I do not have any materialistic desires as I have all the "stuff" I will ever need or desire. However, I believe I can change and improve many people's lives across this great country. You do not have to look hard to find people in need or people who can help others if they just get a financial boost. I hope after you read this book you will pass it on to others who would benefit from my advice or purchase additional copies to give to young people for the same reason.

I realize this is a kind of double give back—I am helping people profit from sound investments and realize their financial goals. I encourage everyone who has been successful to find ways to use their wealth and knowledge to help solve problems for the many people who need help in one way or another.

I learned about the responsibility of prosperity from many of my very generous and helpful clients throughout the years. For example, I had an institutional client who established a scholarship program for young pre-med students around the world who could not afford medical school. I met the person in charge of that foundation around 1995. He did not want anything to do with the stock market and felt strongly that the foundation's funds be invested solely in bonds. Bonds were what he understood and where he wanted to stay. Looking back, bonds were a decent choice at that point because they were paying a reasonable rate of interest of around 7%. I was careful to purchase only highly rated bonds—particularly those attached to federal agencies—which are usually a safe bet and offer a reliable return.

Around 2005, the foundation began to express an interest in investing in the stock market. This was driven largely by a new gentleman in the mix who was a little more experienced across the board. The new leader was from Pennsylvania and had sound investment knowledge because he had worked with other foundations with more diverse portfolios. He pointed out to his bond-friendly colleagues that every foundation in America invested in stocks.

I met with the entire board for the first time in Orlando, Florida, in 2004. There were about 12 doctors at the meeting who had volunteered their valuable time to be there. I was ready to applaud their efforts and devotion to helping people around the world access healthcare, but I found the doctors a bit cantankerous, to put it mildly. There was quite a bit of contention about continuing the policy of investing in bonds versus moving some of those funds into the equity markets.

The first part of the review I provided was for the foundation's current holdings. I quickly pointed out they were generating approximately $364,000 of income from their bond portfolio, which was worth approximately $6.7 million. That return was approximately 5.4%. I brought this to the members' attention because foundations are required to give 5% of the principal value every year. And, given their yield was minimally above 5%, they were barely making the required gifting amount. The concern that I and other members had was if the return was less than 5%, they would be eating into their foundation principle.

I then provided an economic update. I don't think any of us realized at the time how low interest rates would move in the future. I provided information about our consulting services group—the outside portfolio managers we employed to invest in stocks and manage accounts. And finally, I provided information about our outside portfolio managers and the results they achieved over three years, five years, and 10 years. It was certainly my thinking that the foundation needed to make some adjustments in the portfolio on a go-forward basis, and I wanted the board to see I was trying to get them ahead of the curve.

A couple of years later, I provided the board with a proposal for outside managers in the equity space chosen by our investment team from New York. This was our consulting services group—they had the pulse and a mindful eye on each of the managers within their space. The beauty of working with this group was that I knew all the outside money managers had been thoroughly vetted and their track records audited. I also knew if the outside money managers did not measure up in performance or they exhibited a style drift—meaning they were investing outside their space—they would be terminated, and we would replace them with a new manager.

Another aspect of the consulting services group was to provide a recommended group of managers for a client who was looking to invest in all the asset classes of the stock market and have those various categories rebalanced on a periodic basis. What this meant was a client could be confident they were investing in small-, mid-, and large-cap stock in both value and growth segments, and they had an international component in the portfolio as well. The rebalancing that took place involved selling a portion of the portfolios that performed well and adding those proceeds to the portfolios that had not done as well. Talk about a win-win! From my point of view, this made my job much easier because the portfolios they recommended had a strong track record. I would continue meeting with the board and providing reviews on a timely basis.

We started investing in the stock market through these managers. At that point, I recall the account was valued at around $6,000,000 and I told them my goal was to grow the account to $10,000,000. Bear in mind this was a lofty goal because of that 5% of the principal balance a foundation must give each year. For it to grow, the account had to earn more than 5%.

Several years later we reached that $10,000,000 goal. The directors were elated and incredibly grateful for my and my firm's efforts.

They could now make more and larger donations and expand their services to people around the globe. Their intentions were 100% honorable and certainly immensely helpful to many people. I was happy to be helpful to such a worthy cause and be instrumental in expanding their mission.

The good news was their charitable giving was now around $500,000 per year and that certainly made a difference to many more people in need of financial assistance. They would never have reached the goal of $10,000,000 if they stayed in bonds, and the account value would have declined because the bond yields went well below 5%. It was a win-win for all parties concerned!

After my job title and description changed in 2021, I was able to contribute $10,000 to the foundation myself and did so in 2022 and 2023 as well. I told the directors more than once that I was rooting for them, and I proved it with my contributions to their worthwhile organization. They did well by my recommendations and my own investment accounts also did well, which will allow me to contribute to their foundation every year for the foreseeable future. Winning in the investment world can produce some impressive results for everyone. If you approach money with the right attitude, everyone wins.

I have to say this was something I saw firsthand that gave me a tremendous amount of satisfaction—a fulfillment far bigger than just the bottom-line returns. It is one thing to make the rich even richer, but it is an altogether different matter to make an account like this appreciate in value when the money is dedicated to helping others.

Looking back, I am so glad they invested in the stock market as interest rates went down in the coming years. The 7% bonds they invested in early on were yielding around 3% when I retired at the end of 2021. If there is one type of account that should invest in stocks, it's foundations because their time horizon is typically infinite. I have always said the longer the time horizon, the better the odds of getting a good return from investing in the stock market.

In conclusion, without question the stock market will have its ups and downs on a go-forward basis. I believe, however, that given the ever-increasing population of the world and the huge amount of innovation being brought forth from the technology arena—including healthcare and AI—there will be vast amounts of opportunity for investors to place their funds profitably.

If you hang in there through the good times and the bad, this will certainly increase your odds of getting a good return over the long haul and will even put you in a position to contribute to worthwhile causes important to you. Believe me, giving is extremely satisfying and something we should all aspire to do. Everyone needs an investment plan in place to grow their money, not just for their own sake but hopefully—and ultimately—to contribute and help others solve problems in the world.

Golden Strategies

1. Around the globe there is an infinite number of needs to be addressed for the many people who simply lack means. Sadly, no government, even in the best of circumstances, will be able to solve all those needs and problems.
2. As I have grown older and wiser, I have come to fully realize there is more joy in giving than receiving.
3. You can invest your time, energy, advice, and expertise in the same way you contribute money. Always look for ways to give back to the world with the riches you have been blessed with. You may even find your net worth—along with your character—will grow from this experience, and you will relish the sense of well-being!

Workshop Topic

Ask an affluent person what their favorite charity is or choose a cause you are passionate about. Then do some research and get a feel for what the charity's needs are. I suggest visiting them to get clarity on their mission and what they are trying to accomplish. If you feel their goal is worthwhile, figure out how you can best contribute to their cause. I want you to feel just how great it is to help others in your community.

GOLDEN RULE 9

KNOW WHAT YOU OWN

Make Educated Investments

This chapter is the most important one in this book because it encourages you to understand more deeply what you are buying when you invest. It's about making investments with professional money managers guiding you to a better return than you could achieve on your own—with informed consent. This means you don't have to follow your investor's lead blindly. Educate yourself about the trades being made in your name and with your money.

In this chapter I'll teach you a little bit about how to know what you own more deeply, so you can make better informed decisions about your investments.

There are three categories of managed investments you need to be concerned with. They are:

1. Exchange-Traded Funds (ETFs)
2. Mutual Funds
3. Managed Accounts

Each of these three managed investment portfolios has a potential place in your investment account(s). Remember, as I said earlier, you should *own* stocks rather than *buy* stocks. Unless you are willing to devote an inordinate amount of time to managing a portfolio—*and* it's your major hobby—leave the investing to the pros.

Investing in securities is the only area I know of where you can track the performance of the portfolio management team based on their history. Thus, you are given the opportunity to buy into a portfolio with a proven track record, you can track performance, and you can learn something about the companies in your portfolio.

Here are some guidelines for the different kinds of investments you may consider and investigate.

Mutual Funds and ETFs

Another benefit to these kinds of portfolios is you can know what you own. You can look under the hood and see how the engine is functioning. You will know what the portfolio managers are currently investing in. While you may not be able to learn of every investment they make, you will be able to learn of at least the top 10 to 20 investments contained in the portfolio. This also means you will own what you know. If you are uncomfortable with some of the companies the portfolio manager is investing in, there are plenty of alternative managers available for you to consider.

One of the easiest ways to learn what a portfolio manager is currently investing in is to look on the website MorningStar.com. Type in the ticker symbol in the upper left-hand corner and you'll be provided with a fairly good synopsis of what the portfolio manager is currently investing in as well as their track record. This applies both to ETFs and mutual funds.

Which is best for you? The answer to that question may depend upon how much you have available to invest and what type of investment vehicle you are putting your funds into. If you are investing in a 401(k), you will generally be limited to mutual funds and exchange-traded funds. This would also hold true for 529 plans and smaller IRA plans.

Separately managed accounts have higher minimums because the portfolio managers need to be able to diversify the portfolio, which thus creates the need for higher minimum initial investment. I have never seen a 401(k) plan that allows you to invest with a separately managed account manager. Another thing to bear in mind is if you are currently investing in mutual funds, at some point you may want to graduate toward separately managed accounts. This is because they provide greater tax efficiency and the ability to eliminate certain industries or companies from the portfolio entirely.

The two basic flavors of funds are exchange-traded funds, better known as ETFs, and mutual funds. Funds are nothing more than a collection of stocks or bonds or other securities for which the sponsor of the fund pools investors' monies and then manages it in a professional and (hopefully) profitable manner.

Mutual funds historically have been more of the managed style, meaning there is a portfolio manager or management team that will invest in securities based on your objective.

ETFs historically have primarily been tied to a stock index or a particular sector in the economy. This means they may be investing in the style of the S&P 500 or the Dow Jones Industrial Average or the NASDAQ or a sector index like financial stocks or oil stocks.

Lately, the differences between mutual funds and ETFs have become blurred. Mutual funds now offer index funds, and some ETFs are now managed, meaning a portfolio manager buys securities based on their belief of price appreciation rather than buying securities in an established index or sector.

There are currently over 8,000 mutual funds available and the assets under management of these portfolios total over $21 trillion.

The largest mutual fund is the Vanguard Total Stock Market Fund, ticker symbol VTSAX, with approximately $1.3 trillion in that fund. There are currently approximately 7,600 ETFs available with assets totaling approximately $7.74 trillion under management. The largest ETF is the Standard & Poor's 500 index fund listed under the ticker symbol SPY with a total of $400 billion in that portfolio.

Which Is a Better Investment, a Mutual Fund or an ETF?

Both mutual funds and ETFs represent an efficient and straightforward way to invest in securities. One of the major differences between the two is an ETF can be sold throughout the day during market hours.

By contrast, when a mutual fund is sold, it's done at the current closing price at the end of the market trading day, which means you don't really have an exact idea what you will receive when you sell the shares. For example, if you put in your order to sell at 11:00 a.m. Pacific Standard Time, and the market is open for two more hours, there could be a fair amount of difference between the price at 11:00 a.m. and 1:00 p.m.

Another fundamental difference is the minimum amount required to buy these funds. You can buy a single share of an ETF which could be less than $50 whereas a mutual fund would typically require a minimum of at least $250. Also, the management fees for mutual funds are typically higher than ETFs because they require far more oversight.

Another especially important difference between mutual funds and ETFs is ETFs are much more tax efficient. When the portfolio manager of a mutual fund sells shares of stock in that portfolio and incurs a capital gain, shareholders are on the hook for the capital gains tax. The capital gain is passed through to the current shareholders as of the sale date. What's frustrating is if you purchase the fund one day and the portfolio manager sells the shares the next day for a profit, you as a shareholder on the are on the hook for the entire amount of the capital gain.

Funds come in three flavors. They are:

1. Stock funds
2. Bond funds
3. Money market funds

Stock Funds

1. Aggressive Growth Funds

In an aggressive growth fund, you have the potential for greater price appreciation of the share price because you are incurring the most risk. This type of fund will have companies that are the up-and-comers and typically hold equities in the mid-cap space, meaning companies that are not super small but also not household names.

2. Growth Funds

Growth funds have the potential of greater price appreciation because you are still incurring risk, just at a more moderate level than in an aggressive growth fund. This type of fund would typically hold large-cap growth stocks, and most would have a good deal of exposure to technology, including names like Nvidia, Meta, Apple, and Microsoft. This fund would generally be less volatile than the aggressive growth fund, but still more volatile than the growth and income fund outlined below.

3.Growth and Income Funds

These funds typically pay dividends, offer a lower level of risk, and generally do not perform as well as the other two stock funds. However, growth and income funds do have appeal for two reasons. First, you receive current income because you are buying companies that pay dividends. Secondly, volatility is less than with growth and aggressive growth funds. Additionally, the portfolio manager looks for companies with a history of increasing their dividends, so over time your income moves higher. I have seen some growth and income funds actually double the dividend over 10 years, which is why investing in the stock market is often called an inflation hedge.

Bond Funds

1. Tax-Free Bond Funds

These are funds composed of tax free municipal bonds from a specific state or across the nation. The beauty of this type of fund is the income produced is federally tax free. In addition, municipal bonds issued within your state are exempt from state and local taxes too. However, if it is a nationwide fund, you will be on the hook for the income generated to your state. For example, if you live in California and receive $10,000 of income from the fund—but only 10% of that particular portfolio is invested in California bonds—you will pay state income taxes on the $9,000 generated from other states.

2. Corporate Bond Funds

These funds are composed of corporate debt from any number of large-cap companies. These funds are designed to provide an above-average income and most pay income monthly. There are two types of corporate bond funds:

1. Strong credit quality companies. These are companies like Apple that have an incredible ability to pay you interest and principal at maturity.
2. Lower credit quality companies. These are known as junk bonds. Do not invest in these funds. Way too risky. These funds are designed to provide an above-average return but can be very volatile, especially in a slowing economy.

3. Government Bond Funds

Government bond funds are comprised of government securities. The most common are Government National Mortgage Association (GNMA) bond funds which are pools of mortgages backed by the U.S. Government. The risk here is interest rates moving higher. Again, as with corporate bond funds, these are designed to provide monthly income and security of principle. Just be forewarned that the value of your principle will fluctuate inversely with interest rates, meaning if rates mover higher, your value moves lower and vice versa.

Money Market Funds

Money markets are a good idea for your rainy-day emergency money as they typically pay more than bank accounts and liquidity is usually same day if you request a liquidation before the stock market closes 4:00 p.m. EST.

1. Tax-Free Money Markets

A tax-free money market invests in short-term municipal notes. As with municipal bonds, if the securities are purchased within the state you live in, the interest will be tax free.

2. Treasury Money Markets

A treasury money market is the safest. This is because the portfolio manager only buys short-term U.S. Treasuries. Interest is tax free in the state you live in but federally taxable.

3. Corporate Money Markets

This is a money market account composed of corporate securities. The portfolio manager in this instance buys commercial paper from corporations. The maturities on these are less than nine months, so they are a suitable investment for a taxable money market. Bear in mind the money market funds are mutual funds, and as such the manager buys short-term securities to minimize risk. This is because the portfolio manager will always strive to keep the share price at a dollar per share. Be forewarned, however, that some money markets historically have "broken the buck," meaning a security contained within that portfolio did not work out and the share price went below $1. The last time I saw this was in the Great Recession of 2008 and 2009.

Do Not Buy Bond Mutual Funds

While I do not personally like bond mutual funds, I will admit there are two advantages to buying them. First, you do obtain a well-diversified portfolio—more diversified than you can possibly achieve by buying individual bonds on your own. Secondly, you have a professional money manager and/or money management team picking bonds on your behalf, and they will certainly do their absolute best to avoid any credit quality problems for your portfolio. But I strongly believe if you buy individual bonds with strong credit quality, those two advantages become moot.

Disadvantages of Buying a Bond Mutual Fund

1. There is no maturity date on these products, so if interest rates rise, the value of your portfolio will go down. You cannot wait until a maturity date to get your money back, assuming you paid par or 100% for your bond, because there is no date. The only way to get your money out is to sell the fund at the current market value. Be aware, the current market value may never come back to your original investment amount.

   When you own individual bonds and interest rates rise, pushing the portfolio value down, you can always wait until the maturity date or the call date when the values come back to 100%. Another key point is as your bonds get closer to maturity, the values tend to appreciate back to 100%. As an example, if your bond matures in five years and is currently valued at 90%, you will see the bond appreciate at 2% per year.

2. You will pay an ongoing management fee to the portfolio management team. As an example, the Franklin California tax-free income fund A1 share class—which is one of the largest individual state municipal bond funds offered—has a management fee of 0.76. So, over the course of 10 years, you will pay management fees totaling 7.6% to have your portfolio managed.[62] However, if you purchase individual bonds on your own through a financial advisor who specializes in fixed income, you will typically pay 0.5% to 2% for those purchases and no ongoing management fee. Overall, this is a lot cheaper than the 0.75% management fee charge every year.

---

62 "Franklin California Tax-Free Income Fund," Franklin Templeton, June 30, 2024, https://www.franklintempleton.com/forms-literature/download/614-FF.

3. In addition, many bond funds have what they refer to as a front-end sales charge or load. The Franklin fund I just mentioned has a fee of 3.75% for purchases less than $50,000.[63] So, if you look at the management fee plus the front-end sales charge, you can readily see the bond fund is not cost-effective. In addition, if you look at the track record of the Franklin California tax-free fund, it was down 10.13% for calendar year 2022.[64] This was due to the Federal Reserve raising rates through most of 2022. The 10-year average return ending on June 30, 2024, was 2.28%.

There are two yield quotations you want to be familiar with. One is referred to as the distribution yield, which is simply the dollars being paid to you, given the current share price. In other words, if the share price is $10.00 and you are earning 50 cents, the distribution rate would be 5%. The Franklin California tax-free fund has a distribution rate of 3.30%. The second yield you want to be aware of is what is referred to as the SEC yield. This is more complex and can be likened to the yield to maturity on a bond. It equates with the appreciation or depreciation of the total bond portfolio.

The Franklin California tax-free fund has an SEC yield of 3.26%.[65] What this means is you will see gradual depreciation in the value over time. This means some of the bonds in the portfolio are

---

63 "Franklin California Tax Free Income Fund," Franklin Templeton, accessed September 29, 2024, https://www.franklintempleton.com/investments/options/mutual-funds/products/4312/A1/franklin-california-tax-free-income-fund/FKTFX.

64 "Franklin California Tax Free Income Fund Class A1," Fidelity, accessed September 29, 2024, https://fundresearch.fidelity.com/mutual-funds/view-all/352518104.

65 "Franklin Federal Intermediate-Term Tax-Free Income Fund," Franklin Templeton, accessed September 29, 2024, https://www.franklintempleton.com/investments/options/mutual-funds/products/4174/Z/franklin-federal-intermediate-term-tax-free-income-fund/FITZX.

currently valued over 100%. Remember this—all bonds mature at 100%. So, if you take your income every month, which many people do, you will see a gradual decline in the value of the portfolio over time, assuming interest rates stay the same.

The benefit to buying individual bonds is you know exactly what you will earn when you purchase them, assuming you hold them until maturity. If the yield is lower than the coupon, you will see a gradual decrease in the bond value. If your interest rate is lower than the SEC yield or the yield to maturity figure, you will see a gradual appreciation in your portfolio if interest rates stay the same.

If you do not have at least $250,000 to invest in individual bonds I recommend staying away from bond funds in general. I would be more inclined to invest those funds in an equity-based portfolio and let it grow until you reach the $250,000 figure. In other words, try to grow your money now, then convert those funds to income-producing ideas later as you get closer to retirement or are in retirement.

Are Mutual Funds a Thing of the Past?

While mutual funds over the course of time have provided a decent return for investors, I feel at this juncture they are a product of a bygone era and there are better alternatives available. Let me give you three reasons why they are obsolete:

1. Fee structure. The fees for mutual funds can be high, to put it mildly. You may be charged a commission to buy the funds from a full-service brokerage firm and this could be as high as 5.75%. In addition, you will pay a management fee to have your portfolio professionally managed. If it's an international fund that fee may be even higher. The management fee can be as high as 1.5%. In addition, if you are buying from a full-service brokerage firm, you may also pay what is called

a 12b-1 fee which is typically 0.25%. This is the fee paid to the investment firm you bought the fund from and is paid to your financial advisor. This covers the ongoing service for your fund.[66]

2. Another problem with mutual funds is that they are not terribly tax efficient. I know this firsthand because mutual funds I purchased many, many years ago had capital gains from 2021 of over $300,000. Between federal and state taxes, my tax liability was over $100,000. While I've been pleased with the performance of these funds, I stopped contributing to them many years ago because of the enormous amount of taxes they generated from capital gains.

   And on top of that, if I were to sell the funds today, I would again have a huge tax liability. In general, I would say mutual funds are best suited for qualified accounts. Qualified accounts are non taxable accounts like IRAs, 401(k)s, foundation accounts, etc. For 401(k)s, mutual funds are generally your only option.

3. The third major problem I found with mutual funds is when things get scary, investors often run for the door. It's like being in a movie theater when someone yells fire—people get trampled on the way out. The same thing happens with mutual funds. When everybody starts selling their mutual funds, the fund manager is forced to sell securities to raise cash and meet the redemption requests at a very inopportune time. If anything, when the market is down it is a much better time to buy and certainly not to be selling.

---

66 Mike Pappis, "Fees and Expenses on Mutual Funds and ETFs: A Complete Guide to the Often Misunderstood and Hidden Costs of Investments," Boldin, March 14, 2024, https://www.boldin.com/retirement/fees-and-expenses-on-mutual-funds-and-etfs-a-complete-guide-to-the-often-misunderstood-and-hidden-costs-of-investments/.

In that situation, if you are a mutual fund shareholder—even if you are not selling—you will get trampled. The manager is selling securities at the worst possible time, which will hurt your overall performance. Because of these reasons, investors are much better off looking at other avenues for investing their funds. ETFs and separately managed accounts are a much more efficient way to invest over the long term and I feel you will get a much better return.

Separate Managed Accounts

Now we are getting into an area that is my favorite choice for an investor. What is a separate managed account? A separate managed account is one where you have an outside money manager handling your investments based on your risk tolerance, objectives, and time horizon. It is my strong belief a team of investment professionals gives you a much better chance of succeeding in getting you the best possible return rather than a do-it-yourself approach. In my experience I have found very few people have the skill set to manage an equity portfolio.

If you look at firms like BlackRock and other investment firms in this arena, they have teams of research analysts offering advice to the portfolio manager. Research is the key to getting the best return. Hiring a professional investment management team is like hiring a professional sports manager—they can offer and show you the returns on a historical basis, and you can review the management team's results and look at their track record to see just how well they performed. Bear in mind, there is certainly no guarantee the future results will be the same as in the past. But the record does provide an indication as to how your account might perform.

Separate managed accounts are typically available at investment firms across America and around the globe. When I worked at

Merrill Lynch, we had approximately 65 different money managers. They came in all different types and styles that can be grouped into two categories: managers on the equity side of the coin, meaning stocks, and the money managers on the bond side of the coin. The managers came in several flavors as well, meaning they could invest in large-, mid-, and small-cap stocks as well as international stocks. They can be further broken down into growth versus value.

On the bond side of the coin, they are grouped as managers who invest in municipal bonds or corporate bonds. One of the advantages of working with Merrill and other firms like them in the investment world is all our managers were vetted. We made sure they invested funds on a client's behalf in their respective space and provided good returns. If a manager did not perform to their benchmark, they were removed from our platform.

A straightforward way to find out what a specific separate managed account is currently investing in is to type the name of the portfolio into your computer and search online until you come across the name. It may be listed under one of the major investment firms as well if they post information about the portfolios they offer. Look for what is known as the manager profile. This is a succinct sheet outlining a manager's past performance and will include their major holdings and investment objective. If you do invest in a separate managed account, you will know what you own because the positions will appear on your statements as well as online.

So, what does it all cost? The fees can run as high as 3% of the money under management, but a more likely fee is 1.28%.[67] For most of my clients, Merrill charged 1.28%. This was comprised of the manager's fee, which was approximately 0.28% plus the company's

---

67 Katrina Lamb, "Should You Have a Separately Managed Account?," Investopedia, last modified August 31, 2024, https://www.investopedia.com/articles/mutualfund/08/managed-separate-account.asp.

fee of approximately 1%. So, if you invested $1 million in one of these types of accounts you would be paying approximately $13,000 a year in fees. But, if you can average over 10% per year after deducting fees, I think investors would have a very keen interest in that proposition.

The major caveat, of course, is there is no guarantee the portfolio manager can do as well in the future. However, it is indicative of their potential ability to do well. They have a tremendously strong track record when it comes to investing in the stock market, but there are very few guarantees. And, be forewarned you will still pay fees in down markets. In other words, you will pay a fee while you are losing money as not every year produces positive returns in the stock market.

Separate managed accounts are available at most major investment firms. These include J. P. Morgan, Wells Fargo, Morgan Stanley, UBS, RBC, and of course Merrill Lynch. If you inquire about separate managed accounts, the first things the advisor should ask you about are your time horizon, risk tolerance, and need for liquidity. Understanding the time horizon is important because it will determine which course to take. If you're leaning toward investing in equities, you should have at least a five-year window. If your time horizon is shorter, you may want to consider a bond account, either municipal bonds or corporate bonds, depending upon your tax bracket. A municipal bond or corporate bond managed account will have a shorter time horizon, and your risk will be lower. Also, think long and hard about your cash needs. You may have cash needs in the future. This may include starting a business, buying a house, paying an enormous tax bill, and so on.

Advantages of Investing in Separately Managed Accounts

- **Tax efficiency**. Separate managed accounts are much more tax efficient than mutual funds. I can remember tax harvesting at the end of every year to minimize my clients' capital gains. This took a two-pronged approach. If there was a loss in a certain stock, the stock could be sold to realize the loss and help offset the gains in the account for that year. The portfolio manager would have the option to use these proceeds to buy a competing firm in the same asset class or purchase an ETF in the same asset class. This was done to keep the client's money invested.

  At the end of 30 days, the original security could then be repurchased. Thirty days was the rule because if the same security was repurchased before that, it would disallow the loss. This is referred to as a wash-sale rule. Mutual funds manage for total returns and are not as tax efficient for their shareholders.

- **Owning securities outright.** This presents a couple of advantages. First, if there is a significant downturn in the market and redemption requests are flowing into the mutual fund, the fund manager is obligated to sell securities to meet the redemption requests. The portfolio manager is then selling at the worst possible time. If the market is down, you can certainly sell securities in your account if you choose, but you will not be hurt by other investors in the mutual fund because you own the securities outright.

  You can also request certain stocks not be purchased in your account. For example, if you do not want to own tobacco stocks, you can instruct your financial advisor to be sure they do not purchase stocks in that industry.

- **Fees.** Fees in a separate managed account are based on a percentage of the assets within that account. So, the manager will only do better if they perform for you in a positive manner. When the portfolio manager has a poor performance, they will earn less on a go-forward basis. What this means is everyone is on the same page and that limits the possibility of a rogue advisor buying and selling just to generate commissions.

Six Separate Money Managers and Their Track Records

Now that I've discussed separate managed accounts, I want to show you the results of six managers I've picked at random. I've chosen four in the equity space and two in the fixed-income space. All these managers have at least a 10-year track record and you can also see the results on a year-by-year basis over the last 10 years.

The Four Equity Managers Are Listed Below with a Specific Portfolio They Are Managing:

Columbia Threadneedle, headquartered in Boston, Massachusetts, employs approximately 650 investment professionals and is currently managing around $672 billion in assets.[68]

Columbia Management-Dividend Income Strategy. The portfolio manager's strategy is to invest in large-cap stocks both on the value and growth sides. Their emphasis is to identify companies with strong free cash flow that can lead to dividends. They believe companies with capital discipline are more likely to be successful

[68] David Carey, "Columbia Threadneedle," Morningstar, July 16, 2024, https://www.morningstar.com/asset-management-companies/columbia-threadneedle-BN000008GG.

over time.[69]

10-year average return through June 30, 2024: 11.17%

2023 return: 10.79%

2022 return: -4.48%

Top five equity holdings: J. P. Morgan Chase, Microsoft, Broadcom, Exxon Mobil, Johnson & Johnson[70]

Loomis Sayles is headquartered in Boston, Massachusetts, has approximately 840 employees, and is currently managing around $359 billion in assets.[71]

Loomis Sayles Large Cap Growth. The portfolio manager's strategy is to invest in large-cap growth stocks. Their emphasis is to identify high-quality businesses with sustainable competitive advantages and profitable growth.[72]

10-year average return through June 30, 2024: 15.93%

2023 return: 51.69%

2022 return: -27.46%

Top five equity holdings: Nvidia, Meta Platforms, Alphabet,

---

69 "Separately Managed Account Columbia Dividend Income Strategy," Columbia Threadneedle Investments, June 30, 2014, https://www.columbiathreadneedleus.com/binaries/content/assets/cti/public/COLUMBIA_DIVIDEND_INCOME_SMA_FS.PDF.

70 "Columbia Dividend Income Strategy," Columbia Threadneedle Investments, June 30, 2024, https://www.columbiathreadneedleus.com/binaries/content/assets/cti/public/COLUMBIA_DIVIDEND_INCOME_SMA_FS.PDF.

71 "About Us," Loomis, Sayles & Company, accessed October 4, 2024, https://www.loomissayles.com/website/about-us/.

72 "Large Cap Growth," Loomis, Sayles & Company, accessed September 29, 2024, https://gesloomissayles.com/offerings/large-cap-growth/.

Amazon, and Tesla[73]

Riverbridge Partners is headquartered in Minneapolis, Minnesota, has 45 employees,[74] and is currently managing around $11.27 billion in assets.[75]

Riverbridge Partners, LLC-Small/Mid Growth. The portfolio manager primarily invests in the small-cap growth space with an emphasis on finding companies seeking to build both their earnings power and intrinsic value in the long run.

10-year average return through June 30, 2024: 8.56%

2023 return: 20.74%

2022 return: -32.09%

Top five equity holdings: HEICO, Tyler Technologies, Grand Canyon Education, West Pharmaceutical Services, and Globant[76]

Neuberger Berman, LLC is headquartered in New York, New York, has approximately 2,826 employees, and is currently managing around $463 billion in assets.[77]

Neuberger Berman, LLC-International Core. The portfolio manager invests in large cap-value and growth with a smaller emphasis on

73 "Large Cap Growth," Loomis Sayles, June 30, 2024, https://gesloomis-sayles.com/wp-content/uploads/2024/01/LargeCapGrowthComposite-FactSheet.pdf.

74 Riverbridge Partners, email message to the author, October 10, 2024.

75 "Form ADV Part 2A," Riverbridge Partners, LLC, March 15, 2024, https://riverbridge.com/uploads/ADV/Riverbridge_ADV_2A_March_2024.pdf.

76 "SMID Cap Growth Fact Sheet," Riverbridge, June 30, 2024, https://riverbridge.com/uploads/strategies/Riverbridge-Smid-Cap-Growth-Fact-Sheet.PDF.

77 "Neuberger Berman Investment Advisers LLC Client Brochure," Neuberger Berman, March 28, 2024, https://www.nb.com/handlers/documents.ashx?id=b5a8fc44-4ff8-4964-9a9e-e0e5e41accaa.

small-cap value and growth. They invest in equities around the globe with an emphasis on high-quality growing companies that trade at reasonable prices.

10-year average return through June 30, 2024: 5.67%

2023 return: 16.07%

2022 return: -20.9%

Top five equity holdings: ASML Holding, AstraZeneca, Hitachi, Experian, SAP SE[78]

Final Thoughts

There are a couple of important points I want to make here. First, the dividend income strategy from Columbia is one I strongly recommend for investors who are a bit timid about investing in the stock market. What I found over the years is this strategy will not always be number one in terms of return, but it provides a lot less volatility and some current income that can be reinvested into the stock holdings the manager already owns, thus creating a compounding effect. If you look at the return for 2022, -4.48%, while negative, was still much better than the return for most of the other money managers in the equity space.

Secondly, while Loomis Sayles had a better 10-year return, you would need to ask yourself if you can handle the -27.46% loss in 2022. If you are investing for the long term, with a time horizon of over 10 years, you would be advised to invest with a manager like Loomis Sayles. However, if your timeframe is five years, I would recommend a portfolio like the Columbia Management-Dividend Income Strategy. This would hold true for the Riverbridge partners portfolio as well.

---

[78] "Neuberger Berman International ADR Portfolio," Neuberger Berman, 2Q 2024, https://www.nb.com/en/us/separately-managed-accounts.

Lastly, what about Neuberger Berman? The returns for the last 10 years averaged just 5.67%. While they are a good money manager, it is my opinion the international equity space in general did not perform well over the past 10 years for any manager in this space. I do prefer to keep my investments in America and not overseas.

Please note the above returns are gross of fees. This means before any management fees are paid. So, if your fee was around 2%, your overall returns would be around 2% less.

Fixed-Income Managers

Now let's talk about managers who work in the fixed-income arena. Here are two notable examples with long track records that can give you a sense of their performance over time. The beauty in these examples is you know you are dealing with a company that has results over the long term and will be here for the long run.

Nuveen is headquartered in Chicago, Illinois, has more than 3,000 employees,[79] and is currently managing around $1.2 trillion in assets.[80]

Nuveen Asset Management, LLC-Intermediate Maturity. The portfolio consists of high-quality, intermediate maturity municipal bonds with an average maturity ranging from seven to 10 years with emphasis on sector selection, security structure, and issuer credit risk.

10-year average return through June 30,2024: 2.10%

2023 return: 3.90%

2022 return: -8.71%

---

79 "Our People," Nuveen, accessed October 4, 2024, https://nuveen.com/global/about-us/our-people.

80 "Nuveen by the Numbers," Nuveen, accessed October 4, 2024, https://www.nuveen.com/en-us/about-us/about-nuveen/nuveen-by-the-numbers.

Because managed bond portfolios vary dramatically in their holdings, there are no holdings reported.

Pimco is headquartered in Newport Beach, California, just up the street from where I worked as a financial advisor. They have more than 3,150 employees and are currently managing around $1.8 trillion in assets.[81]

Pimco 3–10-year Corporate Ladder. The portfolio consists of corporate bonds ranging in maturity from 3 to 10 years. All are investment grade, meaning BBB or better. Their objective is to minimize default risk and minimize credit downgrades.

10-year average return through December 2023: 2.62%

2023 return: 7.15%.

2022 return: -8.83%[82]

Like Nuveen, this managed bond portfolio does not report their holdings.

Final Thoughts

First, as with the equity managers, the quoted returns are gross of fees and reported with no fees being assessed. Your returns would be lower because of the fees. Secondly, the decade that went from 2013 to the end of 2022 was especially difficult for bond managers. This was because of the extremely low interest-rate environment and rates spiking substantially higher in 2022, thus ending those 10 years with large losses, which extended to the equity managers previously mentioned.

81 "About Us," Pimco, accessed October 4, 2024, https://www.pimco.com/us/en/about-us.

82 "PIMCO-3-11yr Corporate Ladder," Merrill, Q2 2024, https://olui2.fs.ml.com/MLIAP/MLIAPViewDynamicPDF.aspx?IC=199894&PC=FMDN&CC=MER&DT=ManagerProfileColorPDF .

If you had invested in a bond portfolio at the beginning of 2023, I am quite confident you would have done much better over the next 10 years compared to the previous 10 years. It was a much better entry point—the manager was buying bonds at a much higher rate of interest. Both managers are excellent at what they do, but no manager can show spectacular results when the markets are performing poorly.

Golden Strategies

1. Know what you own and develop a simple system for staying current with the performance of your assets.
2. Get comfortable with the different sectors of the stock market as outlined in this chapter and *then* decide which is best for you.
3. When I did my IRA rollover in early 2022, I slowly filtered those funds into a managed account with my daughter Melissa. The funds were invested in 70% large-cap value equities and 30% large-cap growth equities. Looking back, I could have done better had I invested all those funds in large-cap growth, but I still have averaged around 12% per year, so am I happy? You bet! The point is I was lowering my risk and volatility but not eliminating it completely. The bottom line is I was retired so I chose a more conservative route.
4. If you choose to go with a separate managed account, only work with a firm with open architecture. This means they use outside money managers, not their own internal managers. This eliminates potential conflicts of interest because a firm that only uses internal money managers will never fire their own managers for poor performance. When a firm has open architecture, they will constantly review the performance of their managers and if one is not performing, they will be terminated, thus eliminating any conflict of interest.

5. Be sure to review your portfolio quarterly with your financial advisor.
6. Be forewarned that even if you have the best portfolio manager investing your funds for you, when the market moves lower, your portfolio will probably move lower as well. It is very difficult for even the best-performing manager to swim upstream. So don't demand the impossible from your advisors.

Workshop Topics

1. Check out the individual money managers listed in this chapter. Go to company's website and look for the term-managed accounts or separate managed accounts (SMA). Look for the fact sheet. This will provide a wealth of current information that includes their investment performance over the last 10 years along with their top holdings, sector allocation, description of the account, and current emphasis. Look carefully at the year-by-year returns and make sure you are comfortable with those returns. As an example, if you compare the 2022 returns of Columbia Large Cap Growth Strategy and Columbia Dividend Income Strategy, the growth strategy was down -30.42% while the dividend strategy was down -4.48%.[83] Over the long run—meaning 10 years or longer—you will probably earn a better return with the growth strategy. However, buckle in and hold on because it will certainly be more volatile!
2. Check out this website: http://morningstar.com/. I found this site to be my favorite. They provide a wealth of information

83 "Columbia Large Cap Growth Strategy," Columbia Threadneedle Investments, June 30, 2024, https://www.columbiathreadneedleus.com/binaries/content/assets/cti/public/large-cap-growth-sma-strategy-fact-sheet.pdf.

regarding individual stocks, mutual funds, and ETFs. Get familiar with this site as I am confident you will find it very helpful!

GOLDEN RULE 10

IT'S NOT WHAT YOU EARN, IT'S WHAT YOU KEEP

Work with Tax Laws Rather Than Letting Them Work You

If there is just one concept I want you to take from this book, it's that you need to start saving early and contribute to your retirement account every month until you retire. This is especially true given the fact our government has allowed us to make contributions to retirement plans and have those funds grow tax-deferred or even potentially tax free.

This presents a golden opportunity for you, especially if you are young. I encourage you to fully embrace starting a retirement fund sooner rather than later. You will thank me one day. As I promised in my introduction, here is my IRA success story, which I offer in the hope it will inspire you to imagine what is possible for you by just saving a few cents every day.

How I Grew My IRA Account to Over $8.5 Million

I started contributing to my wife's and my IRAs in 1983 after I started working at Smith Barney. In those early years, we were limited to $2,000 per year in contributions. For our simple IRAs way back when, the earnings grew on a tax-deferred basis and were taxable when withdrawn. Back then, the simple IRA was the only retirement plan available. Today you are given opportunities to invest in a whole variety of retirement accounts.

I started contributing to my 401(k) in 1986. Every year from then until I retired at the end of 2021, I maxed out the allowable contribution amount. On top of that, every penny was invested in stocks via the mutual funds that were offered to us for our 401(k) plan. I invested the bulk of my funds in large-cap value and growth stocks. I also invested a smaller portion of those funds in small-cap company funds and a small amount in international funds as well.

Looking back, there were certainly some scary times—even to the point where I wondered what in the hell I was doing. I remember all too well during the Great Recession of 2008 and 2009 when my 401(k) became a 1.8(k). However—and this is a big *however*—I kept contributing to my 401(k) during those scary, scary times! And believe me, I did not sell anything during my entire career!

In other words, I stayed fully invested throughout the entire time of my employment. It would have made perfect sense to sell everything at the beginning of the recession and buy back everything when the recession was over. However, that involves timing the market and I will humbly admit I do not walk on water and I have never met or learned of any human who does—especially when it comes to timing the stock market.

Here are a couple of salient points I want to highlight for you:

1. The earlier you start saving and investing for retirement, the greater the odds of you getting a good return for your investments. What you will find over time is your returns will compound and ultimately give you more money for your nest egg.
2. Why not take a calculated risk by investing your funds in the stock market? After all, if you look at the historical returns of the investments available to you, the mutual funds with the best returns are those invested in the stock market. Without question, those returns prove better in the long run than investing in bonds or even simple money markets. Remember investing in your retirement account is a long-term horizon venture.
3. Never forget the primary goal of saving and investing your funds throughout your working life is to retire without money worries. This will improve the quality of your later life and may even prolong it because stress, and especially financial stress, kills! Hopefully, you will already have started a retirement account and should be on the way to growing your funds to provide you with a wonderful retirement.

I would be remiss if I didn't remind you of two other tax-advantaged investments. For those of you who are close to retirement or in retirement and considering bonds to provide you with current income, I would urge you to consider U.S. Treasuries and municipal bonds as well. Treasuries are state tax free no matter where you live. Municipals are federally tax free no matter where you live—and if you purchase the bonds from the state you live in, they will be state tax free as well.

Another area that allows you some tax advantages is purchasing stocks that pay a qualified dividend. What this means is the federal tax is 20% as opposed to ordinary income tax. This will apply unless you are an individual earning $200,000 or more or are filing jointly earning $250,000, in which case your federal tax on qualified dividends would be 23.8%. The 3.8% difference is for the Affordable Care Act also known as Obamacare. The beauty is this is a lot lower rate than ordinary income tax rates given the maximum federal tax bracket is currently 37%.[84]

Most states tax dividends as ordinary income unless you live in a state income tax-free state. To put this into context, if you are earning a 3% dividend yield, your taxable equivalency in California (assuming the maximum federal tax rate) would be 3.45%. If you invested in a portfolio of dividend-paying stocks with a history of raising dividends, your yield could potentially increase over time. Qualified dividends do not apply to real estate investment trusts (REITS) or master limited partnerships (MLPS).

The bottom line: Take full advantage of the opportunities provided by our tax laws to grow your funds and receive income from your potential bond portfolio.

529 College Saving Plans

A 529 plan provides another wonderful opportunity to grow funds on a tax-advantaged basis. It is designed to help facilitate expenses of college education at a future date. The beauty of a 529 plan is if the funds are used for educational purposes, the growth in those funds is completely tax-deferred—and if they are used for education expenses, the growth portion is also tax free.

A 529 plan has two parties. One is the owner who controls the investments and the other is the beneficiary, the future student. A contribution is made to a 529 plan by the owner or someone else and

84 Nathan Reiff, "What Are Qualified Dividends, and How Are They Taxed?," Investopedia, last modified July 19, 2024, https://www.investopedia.com/terms/q/qualifieddividend.asp.

the funds are invested—hopefully to grow and grow and grow—so it pays for the future student's college education. What an incredible opportunity! As such, I strongly urge you to consider a 529 plan for your children, grandchildren, or other children who could benefit from one of these plans.

There are two basic types of 529 plans: educational savings plans and prepaid tuition plans. Education plans grow the funds tax-deferred, and withdrawals are tax free if the funds are used for educational purposes. Prepaid tuition plans allow the owner to pay for tuition at today's rate for a specific school. You can lock in a lower rate of cost for college expenses as well.

For my clients, we used only the education savings plans. Looking back, the prepaid tuition plans really were not of significance because they tended to lock in the choice of school. Who was to say the student attending college many years down the road would want to attend that university? In addition, there are only eight states that offer the prepaid tuition 529 plan. They are Florida, Maryland, Massachusetts, Michigan, Mississippi, Nevada, and Texas.

What Are the Expenses a 529 Plan Can Pay For?

- Tuition and fees for college, graduate, or vocational schools
- Books and supplies
- Computers, software, and internet access
- Room and board
- College meal plans
- Student loan payments up to $10,000
- Special needs equipment

- Extracurricular activity fees

In addition, if the beneficiary is between kindergarten and high school, a withdrawal from a 529 plan can be made to pay for school expenses with the limitation of $10,000 per year. Bear in mind not all states allow you to use 529 plans for K-12 education. These states include California, Illinois, Michigan, New York, and eight others. In those states, withdrawals for K-12 are federally tax free but state taxable. Withdrawals are totally tax free for qualified college expenses.

How Much Can I Contribute to a 529 Plan?

The total amount that can be contributed to a 529 plan is between $575,000 and $235,000. The state that allows the most is Arizona, which is currently $575,000, and the states that allow the least are Georgia and Mississippi, both at $235,000.[85] Be forewarned that it might be inadvisable to contribute the amounts listed above to a 529 plan all at one time. This is because you would be required to file a gift-tax form—namely IRS form 709.

To maximize the initial contribution, you can contribute $18,000 per year (or $36,000 per year when filing jointly) and you can contribute five times that amount initially, or $90,000 for a single individual and $180,000 for a couple filing jointly.[86] What this means is you can do what is referred to as frontloading, which is an exception to the gift-tax limitation unique to 529 plans. Just remember, by frontloading you are limited from making any further contribution for five years, otherwise you will have to file a gift-tax return.

---

[85] "Find My State's 529 Plan," College Savings Plans Network, accessed October 2, 2024, https://www.collegesavings.org/find-my-states-529-plan.

[86] David Dierking, "529 Plan Contribution Limits in 2024," Investopedia, last modified September 8, 2024, https://www.investopedia.com/articles/personal-finance/010616/529-plan-contribution-limits-2016.asp.

Another strategy is to fund a 529 plan as soon as possible. This will allow the funds to grow over time and potentially have a greater value when they are needed. If I were expecting a grandchild, I would fund a 529 plan as soon as possible after my grandchild was born and has a Social Security number—which the parents can file for as soon as the birth is registered. The website is https://www.ssa.gov/number-card/request-number-first-time. And lastly, four states allow you to deduct the contribution from your state income tax. They are West Virginia, Colorado, South Carolina, and New Mexico. Talk about a win-win!

What If There Is Money Left Over?

If there is money left over after the beneficiary has completed his or her education, you are given several options. First, you can withdraw all the funds. Be warned that there is a 10% penalty for funds withdrawn and not used for educational purposes. In addition, you will be taxed on the growth of those funds. Secondly, you might consider changing the beneficiary. For example, if you have two children and the first child did not use all the funds in the 529 plan for education purposes, you can transfer the remaining funds to your other child. Bear in mind the new beneficiary needs to be related to the original beneficiary.

A third option would be to take the remainder of the funds and put them in a Roth IRA. This plan went into effect January 1, 2024, and was part of the 1.7 trillion 2023 Omnibus funding bill that included several new tax laws. One of the provisions of that bill was to allow leftover funds from a 529 plan to be rolled into a Roth IRA.

There are several restrictions to be aware of before this rollover can be implemented. First, the 529 plan must be at least 15 years old and rollover funds must have been in that account for at least five years. Next, the rollover must be $35,000 or less. The rollover can only be made to the beneficiaries of a Roth IRA. And lastly, the contribution limits for Roth IRAs as mentioned in the previous chapter still apply.

Investment Options

When I was working as an advisor, our 529 plans were composed strictly of mutual funds. Depending on how aggressive the owner wanted to be with those funds, he or she would determine what mutual funds we would recommend. We found the age-based portfolio to be the most efficient. This is best described as a portfolio composed strictly of stocks when the beneficiary is young. Then it gradually converts to a more conservative portfolio—moving from equities to bonds—as the beneficiary gets close to college age. The nice thing about this is the portfolio is on autopilot. This means there is not a lot of oversight required. We did not miss the fact that as the child got closer to 18 years old, we needed to be more conservative.

The bottom line: If possible, be sure to take advantage of the retirement plans mentioned in chapter 2. If you have children or grandchildren, be sure to open a 529 account for their future education. Both vehicles can prove very beneficial. When the government offers such great benefits, utilize them.

Listed below are three key points I want you to think long and hard about. Following these three suggestions will dramatically improve your odds of having a retirement free of money worries.

Golden Strategies

1. If you haven't already started a retirement account, do so as soon as possible! The longer your time horizon, the greater your odds of getting a great return.

2. Do not be afraid to take a little risk, just make sure you can sleep at night.
3. Do not ever touch your retirement assets until you are ready to retire. The penalties are huge, and you lose the future interest income.

Workshop Topics

1. Be sure to keep up to date with current allowable contribution limits for all the various types of retirement and 529 accounts as they will probably increase over time. I suggest this because it's best to contribute the maximum amount you can.
2. Find out if you can have an automatic deduction from your bank account to contribute to these plans on a regular basis as well as the minimum amount to start them.

GOLDEN RULE 11

INVESTOR, KNOW THYSELF!!

Understanding Your Investor Personality Type

What is your risk tolerance? Are you a big spender, or a minimalist? What is your spending style? Can you handle fluctuation in market value? It's important to ask yourself these questions periodically throughout your financial life to keep tabs on yourself, your feelings about savings and expenses, and what money means to you.

Investments never have a straight-line return—risk is always involved. How much fluctuation can you tolerate before you become miserable and anxious? If you are a risk averse person and want a straight-line return, then you are better off with savings accounts at your local bank. Your need for having available funds will play a significant role as well in determining which investment vehicles you choose. So, know yourself and understand your personality type, particularly under the microscope of investing your hard-earned dollars.

I always asked my clients right up front what their liquidity needs were. We took those needs into account with every investment recommendation we made. Different types of business models or lifestyles require unique levels of liquidity. Some people in this California town might not work for months until the next movie comes along. They need more ready cash on hand than my clients with regular paychecks and a steady corporate job.

When it comes to investments—just as in life—time and liquidity are unavoidable, immutable facts that govern the physics of your wealth. The bottom line is it depends upon your objectives. There are five key questions you need to ask yourself. The same questions will more than likely be asked of you when you open an investment account. *Are you trying to grow your money or are you trying to preserve it?*

Your answer to these questions will depend upon your age and how much money you have to invest. If you're comfortable with the accumulation of wealth you've achieved, you may want to lean toward preserving those funds rather than putting them at risk. If, however, you are younger and want to grow your nest egg, then you might be more inclined to invest in areas where you could grow your money.

Personally, I was inclined to grow my money. I never really felt I had enough money to live on in retirement until I reached my mid-sixties. So, I invested most of my funds in the stock market and later purchased municipal bonds as I got closer to retirement.

What Is Your Risk Tolerance?

How much risk can you tolerate? Some people are extremely risk averse—any amount of money on the line will bother them to the point of sleeplessness. If you are like this, you will want to choose safe bets—low-risk investments that won't keep you up at night. Some people are addicted to the thrill of risk, but while I recommend some higher risk when you're still young, be careful not to turn your nest egg into a thrill ride.

Remember this—if you make an investment, you will always have market risk. What this means is the securities you have invested in will fluctuate in value until you sell them or—in the case of a bond portfolio—until the bonds mature or are called. The beauty of securities is they are always very liquid and there will always be a price for them. But you may not like the price on a given day!

Real estate is not nearly as liquid as securities markets. In fact, in trying to sell your home, you may be looking for a buyer for months. Another way to look at risk tolerance is your ability to withstand fluctuation and potential loss of principal in return for the potentially higher return on certain investments.

What Are Your Liquidity Needs and Your Time Horizon?

How much money do you need to keep on hand? How many working years do you have ahead of you, before you retire? How much liquidity do you need to keep your business afloat if you are a business owner? What if you get sick and can't work for a while? I always advised my clients to have two sums of money. The first is what I refer to as rainy-day money. This is money set aside in a Treasury Bill or money market that can be used for emergencies, unforeseen circumstances, and so on.

In my estimation, this is an effective way to extend the time horizon for the second sum of money—the money you have available to invest in the stock market or bond market for which you need a comfort level to deal with fluctuations in market value. The last thing you want is to need funds at an inopportune time and be forced to sell into a bad market, thus guaranteeing loss of your principal.

I remember the recession of 2008 and 2009 all too vividly. Management was telling us to advise our clients to hang in there and not to sell. And, no doubt, they were ultimately right, but try telling someone that at the moment their valuations are dropping through the floor. I had a client who could not take it any longer and sold everything at the worst possible moment. Horribly tough situation, to put it mildly.

These kinds of situations put the financial advisor in an awkward position. Do we say no? And if we do, what if the market falls even lower? The advisor now has a major problem because they have given what can look like bad advice. If the market moves higher, the client rarely appreciates the advice given. It's a no-win situation.

I've always told my clients to have funds available for investment they can put at risk. That way, if the market moves lower, they can make a strategic decision rather than a decision of necessity.

Asset Allocation

Now that you've determined your objectives, let's turn our attention to asset allocation. What is that, you ask? Asset allocation is one of those fancy terms coined by Wall Street. Simply put, it means investing your funds based on your needs and desires. In other words, it cuts to the chase about knowing yourself as an investor. Think long and hard about the questions posed in this chapter and come up with some logical conclusions, because they will direct where your hard-earned money gets invested. In the securities world you have three main classes of investments as outlined below.

1. Stocks: From a historic perspective, stocks have had the highest rate of return. Going back to the 1920s, returns have been around 10% per year. However, without question, stocks are riskier than either bonds or cash.
2. Bonds: Bonds have provided a lower return than stocks. However, they are certainly safer and provide current income.

Your tax bracket will determine whether you purchase taxable or tax-free bonds.

3. Cash: Cash is the safest investment of all. It includes bank deposits, money market accounts, and cash equivalents like short-term Treasury Bills. Cash provides liquidity and allows you to make investments—potentially in both stocks and bonds.

Suggested Asset Allocations Based Upon Age

Let's look at some scenarios and how I would recommend allocating your funds in each situation. Just remember, you are you and I am me, so these are strictly suggestions—do not take them as gospel for your situation.

Single, 22 Years Old, a Long Way to Retirement, and Willing to Take Risk

Max out your 401(k) if you have one and are able. If not, a Roth IRA is suggested. All those funds should be invested in the stock market and allocated accordingly: 50% large-cap, 25% mid-cap, and 25% small-cap.

On the personal side, cash will be dependent on the concept of buying a home at some point. It would be helpful to have a nice cash reserve for any emergencies that arise. Assuming the cash portion is adequate, say at 15%, I would recommend investing the personal funds the same way as I did for the 401(k).

A 32-Year-Old Couple, Married, with a New Baby

Start a 529 plan for the baby. Invest in an age-based portfolio whereby the risk diminishes over time. What this means is, at the beginning, all the funds are invested in the stock market. Then, over time, the percentage gradually decreases so, when the child turns 18, all the funds are invested in the bond market and cash equivalents. It's advisable to max out the contribution to your 401(k) if it's available. Assuming the couple has purchased a home, I would recommend they have the bulk of their funds invested in the stock market. I would have a cash position of 10% and 90% invested in stocks, allocated as with the 22-year-old above.

A 42-Year-Old Couple, Married, with Two Children

At this point, I would hope the couple has 529 plans for their children's education, purchased a home, and, if they can, both are contributing to their 401(k)s or other retirement accounts. For this couple, I would recommend the following asset allocation mix: 65% in stocks broken down as 75% in large-cap and 25% in small- and mid-cap. At this point I would recommend establishing a bond allocation that would be 25% and cash at 10%.

A 52-Year-Old Couple, Married, with Two Children and a Newborn Grandchild

If able, establish a 529 plan for the grandchild. Continue to contribute to the 401(k) plan, again maxing out the contribution. The investment allocation would now begin to change to be a little more conservative—it's advisable to pare back on stock market investments as we get older. The allocation I recommend would be to have 60% in stocks composed of 80% in large-cap and 20% in small- and mid-cap. The bond allocation now would be 25% and the cash position would be 15%.

A 62-Year-Old Married Couple with Children Living on Their Own, Retiring in Five Years

Here I would recommend the following allocation: 35% in stocks with all of it in large-cap, 50% in bonds, and 15% in cash. Again, you can see how the allocation changes to be more conservative as we get older.

A 72-Year-Old Couple, Both Retired

The allocation I recommend would be 20% in stocks, 65% in bonds, and 15% in cash.

Again, these are merely suggestions. In my experience, the answers to the objective questions I asked earlier are of tantamount importance and will ultimately determine where you want to place your funds. Remember, it's about establishing a comfort level so you can sleep at night. That starts with figuring out just what your objectives really are. Many of my clients who had obtained their wealth elsewhere wanted a 90/10 approach meaning 90% in tax-free municipal bonds and 10% in cash.

Portfolio Rebalancing

Here we go with another Wall Street term. Simply put, portfolio rebalancing means moving funds from one asset class to another. A perfect example of this is when an investor pares back their stock portfolio as they age and puts more funds into bonds, which are more conservative.

Another way to look at portfolio balancing is when you take profits from the winning portion(s) of your portfolio and add those funds to the poorer performing asset classes. The challenging thing about this is if you sell your winners, you will have capital gains taxes to pay. However, I found it important to capture those gains while they were there. Profit-taking is a fleeting situation—what's profitable today may not be profitable tomorrow. The fact that we need to be more conservative as we get older warrants reallocating funds.

But again, it all harkens back to knowing yourself. It really is not advisable to have your entire portfolio in stocks when you are 80 years old. You need to ask yourself, "Am I comfortable with the current allocation of my investments?" I further suggest your financial advisor bring up this subject every time you meet.

Golden Strategies

1. The concept of knowing yourself might be one of the hardest concepts to fully grasp. Be honest with yourself about your financial habits, attitudes about money, and tolerance for risk. Knowing yourself is as important as fully understanding and embracing the many nuances of investing.
2. It took me several years to get comfortable with investing in the stock market. Be patient with yourself. Use every opportunity to learn and grow as an investor. Let all this information sink in. Talk to professionals.
3. If you're not comfortable with investing in the stock market because of its ups and downs, I get it. At any moment in time over the last 100 years there have been many factors that could discourage you from investing in stocks. But, if you take time to learn something about the stock market, it may ease your fears and unlock many potential opportunities.

Workshop Topics

1. Ask your friends and family members about their thoughts on investing, particularly regarding risk and time. You will probably find they haven't really thought much about these

aspects of investing, but that will provide further reinforcement that we all need to get on board and start preparing for retirement now rather than later.

2. Think really hard about the following concept and discuss it with your spouse or other family members: Do you want your funds to grow in a straight-line manner—meaning no risk—or are you willing to take some risk? That will mean your funds may not grow every year. Believe me, those years that are down can feel *very* long, to put it mildly. Look at 2022. If you invested in either stocks or bonds that year, you more than likely wound up with less at the end of the year than you started with. Thank goodness 2023 was positive!

GOLDEN RULE 12

TURN YOUR COFFEE INTO GOLD

The Starbucks Savings Strategy

What would you rather have, two cups of Starbucks coffee or $1 million? Apparently, a lot of people in this country are opting for the latte over a financially secure future. As I discussed earlier in the book, a recent article in *USA Today* reported 50% of American families retire with *no* money.[87] In addition, only 26% of American families retire with more than $100,000.[88] Only 3.2% retire with $1 million or more, and only one family in 1,000 has $5 million saved for retirement.[89] My goal for you is to step back and set a goal for yourself of having $1 million or more at retirement.

Here is my plan. Start your retirement program by investing

87 Guynn, "Retirement Savings Crisis."

88 "No Retirement Savings."

89 Ivy Grace, "Can You Guess What Percent Of People Actually Retire With A $2 Million Nest Egg? Here's A Hint – Aim Really Low," Yahoo! Finance, August 23, 2024, https://finance.yahoo.com/news/guess-percent-people-actually-retire-193016661.html.

$5,000 in the ETF ticker symbol SPY. This ETF tracks the performance of the Standard & Poor's 500 index. Then, take $10 a day and add it to the same ETF. This is the same amount of money you would typically spend on two cups of Starbucks coffee. Given the SPY price is around $513, you would be buying a share every month and a half, sometimes earlier or later depending upon the price of SPY.

Also, make sure to reinvest the dividends the ETF generates and buy more shares. You may have to contact a customer service representative from the firm you're dealing with to accomplish this, but it makes a huge amount of difference in the long run in terms of overall returns. This should be done at no charge to you. If your firm charges you for this, find another firm. Simple money markets pay low rates whereas the returns on the Standard & Poor's 500 index are close to 10% historically.

Let's say you're 30 years old today and—though I am sure you don't want to think about it—let's say you plan to retire at 65. This gives you a 35-year window to invest your funds. By using the S&P 500 periodic investment calculator from the amazing website http://dqydj.com/sp-500-periodic-reinvestment-calculator-dividends, you can look back and see what would've happened if you had done what I described above. Starting with $5,000 invested in August 1988, and adding $300 to the SPY ETF monthly, your investment would've grown to the amazing number of $1,013,026.04 by the end of August 2023.

Not bad, considering the initial investment was $5,000 and you added a mere $10 per day. The overall amount you invested was $131,000. That is a return of nearly eight times your original investment dollars. The annualized return was 9.436%. Not bad huh? Two cups of coffee from Starbucks a day versus the potential of having a million dollars at retirement! You can also use the S&P 500 periodic investment calculator to simulate different scenarios depending upon your situation.

Another suggestion is to put this investment into an IRA or, if possible, a Roth IRA. In this way, your funds will grow on a tax-deferred basis. If they are put into a Roth IRA, not only will they grow tax free, but the ultimate distributions will be tax free as well.

When it comes time to take out funds for income, you could invest those funds in bonds. Currently, yields are 5% so if they are at that same level or higher many years from now, that will provide you with around $50,000 of income at retirement.

Implementing this plan is simple. I remember from my old days at Merrill Lynch, if you banked at Bank of America, you could have an automatic deduction from your checking account go to your savings account. As this number grew monthly, you could then transfer those funds online to your Merrill Edge brokerage account and then place the trade online. I'm quite sure other discount firms have similar options available. I also urge you to make sure you place your trades with a firm that does not charge a commission. Currently, most of the discount brokerage firms do not have commission charges for stock trades. Just remember to make sure your dividends are reinvested back into your original investment.

That is my game plan. Study it and implement the idea sooner rather than later. It's simple in nature and easy to accomplish. My goal is for every American family to have at least $1 million saved by retirement.

By now I'm sure you're asking, is there a guarantee? Not a chance, but history does have a way of repeating itself in the market, especially over the long run. Who knows, you might obtain better returns, but maybe not. The real guarantee is if you do nothing, you wind up with nothing—like 50% of American families today.

Simple? Absolutely! Now it is up to you to take the *initiative* to implement this effective plan. Make it your goal to invest $10 a day every day from now until you retire and, believe me, you will not regret it!

Workshop Topic

Check out the website http://dqydj.com/sp-500-periodic-reinvestment-calculator-dividends and run your own calculation with your own numbers. Very worthwhile!

SUMMING IT ALL UP

These 12 points sum up 40 years of experience in the investment world. Use them as a foundation for growing your wealth.

1. Seek out a financial advisor with integrity, knowledge, and experience.
2. Do not be afraid to take a little risk.
3. If you are able, contribute as much as you can to your 401(k). The same holds true for an IRA or Roth IRA. If you are younger, most of your investment funds should be in equities and *not* money markets.
4. Invest in a 529 plan if you have children or grandchildren. This is a fantastic way to save money for a child's education because the growth of those funds is nontaxable if the funds are used for higher education.
5. Always be suspicious and be aware there are fraudsters out there when it comes to investing your money. Make sure you review your monthly statements and don't be afraid to ask your advisor questions. If you are not satisfied with the answers, you may want to talk to your advisor's manager or even your accountant.
6. It may sound a bit trite, but make sure your investments match your risk tolerance. If you can't sleep at night because of your investments, what is the point? And remember, if something sounds too good to be true, it is!

7. Remember, it is time in the market that is your friend, not timing the market.
8. Don't rely on your family and friends to help you with your investment decisions. You need to work with professionals who do this every day.
9. Make sure you thoroughly understand all fees when it comes to investing your funds. Don't be afraid to ask questions.
10. Be aware of elder abuse—in my years of working in the investment arena, I came across several instances of this. It usually takes the form of a younger person taking advantage of and stealing from an elderly person. If you are elderly, trust but verify. Always have a healthy degree of skepticism.
11. Never use margin to buy securities. Always pay for your investments with cash. If the markets go down and you are on the margin, you may be faced with a margin call and need to raise cash. This forces you to sell your securities at the most inopportune time to meet the margin call.
12. Finally, stay away, stay away, stay away from cryptocurrency. Way too risky!!

EPILOGUE

Gratitude Is Golden

Dear Reader,

I felt it appropriate to close out my book with a philosophy I have come to embrace that has contributed immensely to my life. It's the concept of being grateful. I have enjoyed a very blessed life, and I can't help but feel there are forces out there that have brought me so many riches—not just monetary riches, but the riches of family and friends. As I look back, I stand in awe of how life has treated me so well. I feel I won the lottery.

I used to play the lottery frequently. I thought to myself, wow, if I won the lottery—things would be amazing. Then one day it hit me: If I won the lottery what would I do with the money? Would I buy a new house? No. Would I buy a new car? Maybe, but probably not. A vacation home? Not necessarily. And I realized, I'd already won the lottery. But I won a much more important lottery. I won the lottery of life! I fervently believe my philosophy of being grateful for so many years has had a profound influence on all aspects of my life.

Thus, I would urge you to express gratitude and be appreciative for everything you have. My form of gratitude took the form of prayer, which I believe really multiplied my riches. I can remember people asking me, "How are you doing?" And, of course, my retort was, "Living the dream." The irony was I *was* living *the dream* and still am.

So, I will leave you with the saying I read to my clients at my retirement celebration. It's an original saying from yours truly.

Live each day filled with gratitude!

Be grateful! For the more grateful you are, the more things you have to be grateful for. The more things you have to be grateful for, the more grateful you become. And the more grateful you become, the more grateful you are.

That to me completes the perfect circle, the perfect circle of life, and I believe strongly that if you embrace this philosophy, it will help you in all aspects of your life! After all, gratitude is golden!

Transition your journey in life from a journey of ambition to a journey of gratitude.

I wish you nothing but the absolute best in terms of your investments and I hope you will achieve more than you ever dreamed of!!!

All the best!

ACKNOWLEDGMENTS

There are three people who guided and assisted me in writing this book and I wish to acknowledge them.

Beverly West, my editor, who brought my concepts to life and provided greater clarity to the many nuances of money and investments.

Nathan McMahon, my wife's nephew who provided the technical support that was so helpful in preparing this book.

Dr. Neal Pepper, my investment professor at California State University, Northridge. His first words to our class were: "There is no such thing as a free lunch."

I am profoundly grateful to these fine people.

BIOGRAPHY

Frank Buchholz retired from the financial services industry at the end of 2021 after working with affluent clients for 40 years. He started at Smith Barney and transitioned to Security Pacific Bank. In 1991, Bank of America merged with Security Pacific. He later joined Merrill Lynch after Bank of America acquired them in the fall of 2008. Frank worked with many great clients from Orange County, California, and other parts of the country as well. He received numerous awards while working at Bank of America and Merrill Lynch. His specialty was municipal bonds as well as equities. After 40 years, Frank can honestly say he has pretty much seen it all.

www.ingramcontent.com/pod-product-compliance
Lightning Source LLC
LaVergne TN
LVHW052319200926
848481LV00002B/606
9798992064001